Pooh *and the* Philosophers

John Tyerman Williams is a Doctor of Philosophy and lectures on theatre, English literature and English history. His career began at the age of fourteen, playing Emil in the film of *Emil and the Detectives*. After working as a professional actor, he taught for many years and returned to Oxford in his sixties, receiving his doctorate for a thesis entitled 'Bearers of Moral and Spiritual Values: The social roles of clergymen and women in Britain, c. 1790 – c.1880 as mirrored in attitudes to them as fox-hunters'. He lives in Cornwall.

Pooh and the Philosophers is now an international bestseller and has been translated into thirteen languages. It was followed by John Tyerman Williams' other book on Pooh, now entitled *Pooh and the Magicians*, which reveals the Great Bear as a master of occult wisdom.

Pooh and the Philosophers

JOHN TYERMAN WILLIAMS

with illustrations by Ernest H. Shepard

EGMONT

First published in hardback in Great Britain 1995
by Methuen, London
This paperback edition first published 1997
Reissued 2003 by Egmont Books Ltd,
239 Kensington High Street, London W8 6SA

A CIP catalogue record for this title is
available from the British Library

ISBN 1 4052 0517 2

1 3 5 7 9 10 8 6 4 2

Printed and bound in Great Britain
by Cox & Wyman Ltd, Reading, Berkshire

To Elizabeth Mapstone
whose encouragement and constructive criticism
turned a casual joke into this book

Acknowledgements

I owe much to those who gave time and thought to reading and commenting on the text. To Michael Lockwood, Lecturer in Philosophy at Oxford University, I owe a very special debt for giving me the benefit of his expertise and saving me from several errors. Sarah Lumley-Smith, who sustained my interest in philosophy over many years, also made valuable suggestions. Michael Abbott made some important corrections. For any remaining errors, I, of course, am solely responsible. I should also like to thank that dedicated mainstream Ursinologist, Akita Grinnall, for stimulating my interest in the Great Bear. Finally, I should like to express my gratitude to my publisher Geoffrey Strachan, for his encouragement, and to my copy editor, Georgina Allen, for her vigilance. Both also made valuable suggestions for improving the text.

Contents

1

What this book is about

A. N. Whitehead told us that the European philosophical tradition 'consists in a series of footnotes to Plato'. And he was partly right. All we need to do is to delete 'Plato', insert 'Winnie-the-Pooh', and change 'a series of footnotes' to 'a series of introductions'. This work will demonstrate beyond all reasonable doubt, that the whole of Western philosophy – including of course Plato himself – is best considered as a long preparation for Winnie-the-Pooh. Philosophy *since* Winnie-the-Pooh does naturally consist of footnotes to '*that* sort of Bear'.

Ever since the publication of Frederick C. Crews's *The Pooh Perplex* in 1979, and of Benjamin Hoff's *The Tao of Pooh* (1982) and *The Te of Piglet* (1992), we have known that *Winnie-the-Pooh* was no mere children's classic, unless, of course, we take it as an example of truths hidden from the wise and revealed to babes and sucklings.

Crews's great pioneer work established our text as one of profound depth and almost indefinitely extended meaning; a text that richly repaid examination by the most varied – and indeed often the most contradictory – techniques that modern scholarship, criticism and theory could provide.

These approaches, wide-ranging though they were, still left the Pooh corpus open to the charge of ethnocentrism. Benjamin Hoff delivered it from this accusation by revealing that the 'Bear of Very Little Brain' strikingly illustrated the Eastern Way of Lao-Tse.

So far as I know, no scholar has yet shown that this many-layered text speaks equally for African and Indian, for Australian Aboriginal and Amerindian cultures. But this can only be a matter of time, and, no doubt, of giving due weight to the roles of Tigger, of Kanga and of Roo. Obviously too the work is a sustained denial of speciesism.

Meanwhile our immediate and richly rewarding task is to explore the wealth of *Winnie-the-Pooh* and *The House at Pooh Corner* within the context of Western philosophy. Before we get to grips with our subject, a few preliminary remarks are in order.

First, there may be some who object that Pooh is repeatedly referred to as 'a bear of very little brain';

more exactly, as 'a Bear of Very Little Brain', the size of the capitals emphasizing the smallness of the brain. At first sight, this may seem a serious objection to our claim that he is a great philosopher. Nor can we dismiss it as the mere envy or incomprehension of lesser minds, though it often was precisely that. But on several occasions, Pooh himself explicitly accepts this description.

Fortunately the explanation is simple. In describing himself as a Bear of Very Little Brain, Pooh is merely continuing the tradition of Socrates, who constantly professed to be an ignorant enquirer. Pooh's profession of stupidity, like Socrates' profession of ignorance, was obviously a mask, and the mask sometimes slipped. In his 'Anxious Pooh Song', he proclaims the truth:

> Pooh was a Bear of Enormous Brain
> (*Just say it again!*)
> Of enormous brain –

This study will show how well justified that claim was, while still leaving vast areas of that enormous brain to be explored in the future.

Secondly, though Pooh himself is the greatest representative of philosophy, he is not the only one within the *Pooh* texts. Eeyore clearly represents the Stoic tradition, and – this will surprise many – is the key to a whole section of Nietzsche's *Thus*

Spake Zarathustra. Piglet is rich in allusions to moral philosophy. Owl is, among other things, a lively satire on the sort of academic philosophy that prides itself on its detachment from everyday life. Tigger's search for breakfast demonstrates the importance of secondary motives in John Stuart Mill's more sophisticated version of Utilitarianism.

Thirdly, our readers may have wondered how two fairly short books could really contain the whole of Western philosophy. They may even have suspected this claim was not wholly serious. It was serious, and it is justified. What enabled A. A. Milne to compress so much into so little space was his constant use of the same incident to illustrate several philosophies. We shall find this over and over again in the course of our Ursinian studies.

The following chapters will show in detail why we say that all but the most recent of Western philosophy can best be seen as a vast preparation for Winnie-the-Pooh.

2

Pooh and
Ancient Greece

The Greek cosmologists

All students of Pooh are familiar with his balloon adventure in Chapter One and with his gift of 'a Useful Pot' to Eeyore in Chapter Six. All students of early Greek cosmology will remember that Anaximander put forward the theory that the earth was shaped like a cylinder, while Pythagoras, like Aristotle later, held it was round. So far, however, philosophers have disgracefully neglected the clear connections between these well-known facts. Second only, of course, to the disinterested search for truth, no task is more pleasing to scholars than exposing the negligence, ignorance and stupidity of their fellows. To both these pleasures we now address ourselves.

Pooh and
the Philosophers

Let us first recall the balloon incident. It began when Winnie-the-Pooh asked Christopher Robin if he had a balloon, and Christopher Robin asked why he wanted one.

> Winnie-the-Pooh looked round to see that nobody was listening, put his paw to his mouth, and said in a deep whisper: 'Honey!'

Pooh Bear's secrecy alone should alert us that something more than mere material honey is in question. Everyone who knew him at all must have known his typically bearlike passion for that sweet substance. So why the secrecy?

Hasty thinkers may jump to the obvious conclusion that Winnie-the-Pooh was simply anxious to keep this particular honey to himself. Alas! It is just such superficial reading that has blinded generations to the true depth of Milne's great work and denied him his proper place beside Plato. For he indeed is to Pooh Bear as Plato is to Socrates.

A very little thought is enough to show how implausible it is to interpret 'honey' in this context in its everyday sense. Why should Winnie-the-Pooh take such elaborate precautions to protect honey that was so difficult to reach? On the material level, even he, with the help of a balloon, failed to get any.

What then is the deeper meaning of 'honey'? What was Winnie-the-Pooh really seeking?

It is no surprise to find our question answered, partly at least, in St Matthew's Gospel, which tells us that John the Baptist fed on 'locusts and wild honey'; in Dean Swift, who associates honey with 'the two noblest of things, which are sweetness and light'; and in the hymn that describes the heavenly Jerusalem as 'with milk and honey blest'.

These quotations – chosen out of many – make it clear that there was an ancient and persisting tradition which made honey a symbol either of some spiritual quest, as in St John's case, or the reward of the successful questor, as in the other examples.

Readers who are more familiar with 'sweetness and light' in Matthew Arnold than in Swift will find it easy to apply them to Pooh Bear, who spread these admirable qualities around wherever he went.

It is not our purpose here to examine the question of Winnie-the-Pooh's spirituality or his claims to sanctity. The case for his canonization is at too early and delicate a stage for that to be appropriate. For the moment, it is enough to say Hoff has clearly demonstrated that Pooh Bear has achieved Enlightenment by listening to the voice within. We remember too that Socrates, whose similarity to the Bear we shall repeatedly recognize, has often been regarded as a mystic.

Here, though, we are concerned with Pooh the philosopher, and so we can state confidently that the primary meaning of 'honey' in this parable is philosophic truth.

So far, we have concentrated on the symbolism of the honey, but of course the balloon is equally important. We have already hinted that here it symbolizes the earth. Let us now explore this idea to learn something of its full richness.

The shape of the balloon makes the elementary symbolism obvious enough, while the picture of the balloon floating in the air is as near to the earth floating in space as the imaginative limits of this parable allow. Nevertheless, this picture prompts some questions. It even raises what the shallow-minded may consider difficulties.

If, such people may object, we do, for the sake of argument, accept this rather wild theory of a hidden meaning, then surely this incident shows that Winnie-the-Pooh spectacularly failed in his quest for truth. For he did not gain the honey, and Christopher Robin had to rescue him by shooting the balloon – and Pooh Bear – down.

What, others may ask, is the connection between the shape of the earth and philosophic truth? Isn't this confusing philosophy with astronomy?

To answer the second question first, may we point out that the separation of science from philosophy is comparatively recent. Well into modern times what we now call 'science' was named 'natural philosophy'. The very earliest Greek philosophers were cosmologists, that is, enquirers about the nature of the universe. How did it begin? What was it made of? What were the stars and planets? How far off were they? *What shape was the earth?*

Remembering, as we must always remember, that Winnie-the-Pooh was a philosopher in a truly universal sense, we can see it was perfectly natural that he should concern himself with cosmology. He would not be the unique phenomenon that he is, if he did not encapsulate the whole of Western philosophy.

The intelligent reader will already have realized the Bear was here reminding us that at some time between 550 and 500 BC Pythagoreans taught that the earth was round and revolved round a central fire. Two centuries later, Aristotle repeated that the earth was round, though he regarded it as stationary, and placed in the centre of the universe. And it was Aristotle's picture that was accepted by most educated Europeans until the seventeenth century, when the sun-centred system of Copernicus and Galileo took its place.

When we turn to the first objection, we must frankly admit a more real difficulty. The story of Pooh Bear, the balloon and the honey does seem to show him failing in his quest. So how should we proceed?

By now, the perceptive reader will feel every

confidence in our ability to find an allegorical interpretation, and the perceptive reader will be right.
There are several interpretations, but they do not all
fit easily together. We will select the more obvious
ones and discuss the problems arising. Finally we
will suggest a solution.

1. The first interpretation is that Pooh Bear is here
warning us that the philosopher's task is long and
arduous. If we attempt this task, we must not expect
our first endeavours to lead us to our goal. It is
significant that a great contemporary philosopher,
Sir Karl Popper, called his autobiography *Unended
Quest*. We must be prepared for disappointments.
Inevitably, especially in the early stages, these disappointments will make us downcast, just as our
exemplar was literally cast down to earth.

In its own way, the quest for truth demands as
much courage as the quest for the North Pole. Our
hero rose from the earth and continued his search
until he found the North Pole (Chapter Eight). In
this, as in so many ways, he is our moral as well
as our intellectual guide.

2. The second explanation is similar to the first, but
more precise and concrete. Whereas the first was a
general warning about the philosopher's difficulties,
the second is particularly concerned with science or
natural philosophy. Consider Pooh's words explaining why he wants to come down.

> *'These are the wrong sort of bees . . . So I*
> should think they would make the wrong
> sort of honey.'

Pooh Bear had set out to bring honey (truth) and the balloon (the hypothesis that the earth was a sphere) together. That is, to demonstrate the truth of the round-earth hypothesis. What then made him recoil? Pooh himself tells us quite explicitly: he discovered that the bees that made this honey were *'the wrong sort of bees'*, and he deduced they would therefore make 'the wrong sort of honey'.

Something in his original hypothesis was incorrect. Obviously not that the earth was round. That, we know, was correct. What then? Something to do with the bees.

What was it that made him decide these bees were the wrong sort? His decision came immediately after we learn –

> One bee sat down on the nose of the cloud
> [i.e., Winnie-the-Pooh's nose] for a moment,
> and then got up again.
> 'Christopher – *ow!* – Robin,' called out the
> cloud.

In this situation, the only reasonable explanation of *'ow!'* is that the bee had stung Winnie-the-Pooh's

---

nose. Now if we ask any qualified person – in this case, anyone who has been stung by a bee – what did that person feel when stung? the answer will be, 'I felt a burning sensation.'

Precisely: a burning sensation. And what is the usual cause of burning? Fire. And this of course brings us straight back to the Pythagoreans, and a serious error in their picture of the universe.

For when they said that the earth revolved round a central fire, they did not mean the sun. According to Pythagoras, or probably his later followers, the sun itself, like the earth and other heavenly bodies, revolved round this central fire, which they called the Altar of Zeus. No human ever saw this fire, they explained, because the inhabited parts of the globe were always turned away from it.

So when Pooh Bear experienced the burning pain of a bee sting, this symbolized the philosophical pain of discarding a cherished hypothesis. We note the unhesitating courage with which he performed this painful duty.

We also see how great his anguish was when we go on to read 'his arms were so stiff from holding on to the string of the balloon all that time that they stayed up straight in the air for more than a week.' What a brilliant picture of the way in which habit and emotion may cling to a belief that evidence and reason have rejected!

But here you may object that Pooh seems to have

over-reacted, abandoning the round-earth hypothesis as well as the Pythagorean fire. For how else can we understand the shot-down balloon?

Here we come to a central problem, which will meet us again and again in our study. How far dare we probe into that Enormous Brain, and – an even more delicate matter – can we claim any insight into the feelings of its owner? In this particular case, is it not an impertinent intrusion to speculate on his emotions at the moment his hopes, like his balloon, collapsed?

Such scruples do credit to the delicacy of those who feel them, but I think they are misguided. Indeed, with the best will in the world, they are no compliment to Pooh, for they imply that he himself suffered the limited knowledge of the philosophers he expounds and explains. Can any serious Ursinologist (student of the Great Bear) believe that our universal philosopher was, even for a moment, deceived by the Pythagorean error?

Certainly not. He was not *experiencing* error and anguish but *demonstrating* them for the benefit of us, his readers, who are less well informed. So even if we take the deflated balloon to mean the (temporary) abandonment of the spherical-earth theory, he was not discarding it himself, but merely warning us not to discard a whole theory just because there are valid objections to part of it.

3. Readers may be wondering why we have said hardly anything so far about Christopher Robin. His part is crucial in our third interpretation. Moreover it throws new and possibly surprising light on his function in the entire work.

The key lies in a most revealing statement that Christopher Robin makes to the narrator, just after the balloon and honey incident:

> 'Pooh couldn't [catch the Heffalump], because
> he hasn't any brain.'

This shows us, very early on, that Christopher Robin is totally incapable of appreciating the Great Mind he is privileged to know. This should alert us to the fact that his role is to represent the ordinary, commonplace mind, thoroughly satisfied with its own narrow limits and its equally narrow world.

We must not be too hard on him. He has his virtues. He is kind and friendly, even if rather patronizing. But he is simply not in the same intellectual league as Winnie-the-Pooh. Even the education he disappears into at the end is probably the conventional upper-middle-class kind, more likely to confirm his limitations than to broaden or deepen his mind.

It is no surprise then to find him completely failing to understand the meaning of what is going on before his eyes. He even takes at its face value

Pooh's joke that he intends to deceive the bees into taking his muddied body for a black cloud under the blue sky of the balloon.

Pooh has obviously chosen an infantile joke as most suitable for Christopher Robin, but he must have been astonished to find it was taken seriously. He tests his earthbound friend, asking,

> 'What do I look like?'
> 'You look like a bear holding on to a balloon.'
> 'Not,' said Pooh anxiously, ' – not like a small black cloud in a blue sky?'
> 'Not very much.'

No wonder Pooh Bear asked his second question 'anxiously'. We can imagine his fading hope that his friend would think again, think more deeply, and not respond with well-meaning but feeble literalism.

There are of course many more possible interpretations of the incident we have begun to explore. Some we shall meet in later chapters. Others we leave as a joyful task for our readers. All we wish to say now is this:

1. We have clearly shown that Winnie-the-Pooh may choose to teach us by enacting the roles of many different philosophers and demonstrating their particular teachings. Thus acting on the

---

Zen proverb 'One showing is worth a thousand sayings.'

2. So we must be prepared to find him using this technique again. This will put us on our guard not to be hasty in making up our minds about the merits of whatever particular theory is presented at any given time.

3. Equally, we must be cautious of assuming that our teacher holds the particular view he is presently expounding.

4. It follows that we shall often meet very different and even contradictory views.

5. We must distinguish between expounding contradictory views and being aware of several different levels of meaning.

Naturally, we shall call attention to these points whenever necessary, but readers will find it helpful to keep them constantly in mind.

This advice is particularly appropriate when we turn to Winnie-the-Pooh's birthday present to Eeyore, as described in Chapter Six of *Winnie-the-Pooh*.

The chapter begins with Eeyore in even more than his usual gloom. When Pooh asks him why, Eeyore's first answers are obscure and confused. Pooh immediately responds with his Socratic pretence of ignorance. As with Socrates, the purpose

---

of Pooh's questions is not to inform himself, but to make his companion clarify his ideas.

His questions soon bring the following facts to light. It is Eeyore's birthday. He has had no presents, no birthday cake. 'No proper notice taken of me at all.'

The kindly Bear acts immediately to comfort Eeyore. He hurries home to find him a present. When he meets Piglet, he urges him to give a present too. Pooh first decides to give Eeyore 'quite a small jar of honey', and encourages Piglet's suggestion that he should give a balloon.

It is almost incredible that anyone could fail to notice the renewed connection between honey and a balloon and to draw the obvious conclusions. It is no credit to scholarship that we must record that this failure has been universal.

Devoted, even if superficial, readers will remember that neither present reached Eeyore quite as originally planned. Piglet fell on his balloon and burst it. Pooh himself ate all the honey on the way.

At this stage, those of little faith might be tempted to join the Christopher Robins of this world, and judge Pooh was at best a well-intentioned blunderer. They might even condemn him as selfish and greedy, and think that giving Eeyore the empty jar and calling it 'a Useful Pot' was feeble if not hypocritical. They suppose that Eeyore would end up sadder than ever.

But how *does* he end? He is delighted to discover that he can put the remains of the balloon into the Useful Pot and take them out again. Piglet speaks to him. 'But Eeyore wasn't listening. He was taking the balloon out, and putting it back again, as happy as could be . . .'

How do we interpret this incident in the light of what we already know about the symbolism of honey and balloon? Let us look first at the undoubted facts.

1. Eeyore was happy.
2. He was 'as happy as could be'.
3. This happiness was the result of the presents he had received.

The statement that he was as happy as could be needs careful attention. It is such an everyday phrase to express a high degree of happiness that it is all too easy to overlook its precise meaning here.

In philosophical works, we should expect to find words used with rigorous exactness, and Milne never fails to do so. So we must interpret this statement to mean that Eeyore was as happy as his nature made it possible for him to be. We do not all have the same capacity for happiness. Different things make different people happy. In other words, the presents he received were perfectly suited to him, though they might have been totally unsuited to someone else.

Even on the material level, honey would not have been particularly acceptable. We know from Chapter Two of *The House at Pooh Corner* that his favourite food was thistles. He even tells us himself that he was keeping a particularly juicy thistle patch for his birthday.

This still leaves us looking for a deeper meaning and it is not hard to find. Eeyore was clearly in capable of receiving philosophic or scientific truth. To force it on him would have been positively unkind. After short consideration, Pooh realized that his original intention of giving Eeyore the honey of Truth was inappropriate, and acted accordingly.

So what do we make of the Useful Pot? Here, not for the first or last time, E. H. Shepard's superb drawings are essential to an understanding of the text. He shows us a roughly cylindrical Pot whose height was greater than its diameter. What cosmological theory does this suggest?

At once we remember Anaximander of Miletus, who early in the sixth century declared that the earth was a short cylinder, 'like the drum of a pillar'. When we ponder on this fact and its implications, we are struck with admiration for Pooh's profound skill as a teacher.

He realized that such a simple mind as Eeyore's could not accept the heliocentric theory at once. He must be brought to it step by step. He must, in fact, be led to recapitulate the history of cosmological theory – in simplified form, of course. How better to start him than with this early theory of Anaximander? The Pot was a solid object which Eeyore could see and touch. His physical grasp of the Pot would enable him eventually to grasp the theory mentally. This in turn would serve as a launch pad for his mental journey to the truth.

The deflation of the balloon suggests the difficulty Eeyore would have had in accepting a spherical earth at this stage of his intellectual development. His happiness in putting the deflated balloon in and out of the Useful Pot proves Pooh's exquisite tact and judgment in fitting gift to receiver. For by playing with these two theories of the world Eeyore was learning to move in his own time and when he was ready from the incorrect to the true picture.

We can be sure that one day he will take the balloon out and not put it back again, and, in thought if not in act, inflate it in token that he has arrived at the truth. A truth he could not have accepted in any other way. And now we see the true usefulness of the Useful Pot.

Pooh and Plato

The references we have made to Pooh's assumption of the Socratic mask of ignorance have naturally made our readers wonder what Winnie-the-Pooh has to tell us about Plato. Let us look at a passage which at first seems remote from the great Greek. Its relevance will soon be plain.

One morning, on his way to visit Christopher Robin, Pooh Bear is composing a new song. The first line comes easily –

Sing Ho! for the life of a Bear!

Then he is briefly stuck, but inspiration comes, and he quickly produces a complicated nine-line stanza. The last line goes –

And I'll have a little something in an hour or two!

'He was so pleased with this song that he sang it all the way to the top of the forest.' It then strikes him – and this is the vital Platonic connection – that he will be having 'the little something' in much less than an hour, and so the last line will not be true.

Now one of the best-known facts about Plato is that he excluded poets from his ideal Republic mainly because they told lies (*Republic*, Books Two and Three). So what does Pooh Bear do? As soon as he realizes the last line is not true, he turns it into a hum.

Now Plato himself admitted, in Book Ten of the *Republic*, 'that poetry should return, if she can make her defence in lyric or other metre.' This is exactly what Pooh has done. He dropped the offending line the moment he saw it was no longer true. That was negative defence, removing anything that Plato could reasonably object to. Then he hummed, thus hinting that poetry could defend itself 'in lyric or other metre', a hint he develops fully in many other places.

So in one short passage, Winnie-the-Pooh has admitted the partial justification of Plato's criticism, but shown that it is partial. And he has answered Plato on his own ground, by showing that poetry can make just the sort of defence that Plato admitted he would accept. As Plato himself pretty clearly did not believe this defence was really possible, Pooh's solution shows he could understand and appreciate all Plato had to offer, and then go beyond it. In short, Pooh includes all Plato, whereas Plato includes only part of Pooh.

We must not think that our author placed this incident of the song at random. He placed it at the beginning of the chapter entitled 'The Expotition to the North Pole' because this is the chapter richest in Platonic thought.

The next important Platonic reference in this chapter occurs just after the episode of the song. Pooh finds Christopher Robin preparing for an Expedition (or Expotition) to the North Pole. Leaving aside another example of Pooh's Socratic pretence of ignorance, let us concentrate on the striking fact that in the short space of seventeen lines we find no fewer than seven 'x's.

Now 'x' is one of the rarest letters in English. We need not go into elaborate calculations to prove that an average of one 'x' per 2.43 lines is quite exceptional. The x-frequency, if we may name it thus, is even more remarkable when we exclude a passage of nine x-less lines between the fifth and sixth examples. Then we have the truly staggering concentration of seven 'x's in nine lines: an average of one 'x' per 1.29 lines. (All calculations to two decimal places.)

A mere coincidence, does anyone suggest? An inevitable result of the fact than an expedition is the subject of their conversation? Reader, remember that we are studying the supreme work of Western philosophy. Not one word, not one letter, not one comma is there by chance. Everything in it has a meaning. Indeed that is an understatement. Everything in it has several meanings.

Notice the way in which our author calls our attention specially to this letter. When Pooh asks,

'Where are we going to on this Expotition?'

Christopher Robin answers,

> 'Expedition, silly old Bear. It's got an "x" in it.'

It is incredible but true that up till now Pooh scholars have either ignored this crucial passage or taken it as a joke. Not one has asked why Christopher Robin corrects 'Expotition' to 'Expedition' – a matter of changing 'ot' to 'ed' – and then calls our attention to 'x', which was equally present in both versions. And two pages later, Pooh explains 'Expotition' to Piglet just as something that has an 'x'.

What does this signpost point to? What does 'x' mean to us? First and foremost it is the unknown quantity. This fits well enough when the subject is an expedition into the unknown in search of the unknown. But this is only the first step. We need another to lead us directly to Plato. What is it?

Plato was a master of the general and the abstract rather than the particular and the concrete. Therefore we can hardly be wrong if we expand the meaning of 'x' from the particular 'unknown quantity' to the more general 'mathematical symbol'.

Everything now falls into place. We remember it was Plato who inscribed over the door of his Academy the words 'Let no one ignorant of Mathematics enter here'. This naturally followed the well-known connection of Platonism with the teachings of the

Pythagorean School. And an essential Pythagorean doctrine was that the universe had a mathematical basis – a brilliant anticipation of some theories of modern sub-atomic physicists.

We can now see that the Expotition to the North Pole is an allegory of the search for the ultimate structure of the universe. No longer can we be surprised that it was Winnie-the-Pooh who discovered it.

We notice also Milne's skill in combining the history of philosophy with his allegory. For it illustrates the continuing close relationship of cosmology with metaphysics, ethics and epistemology (theory of knowledge).

As we have recently emphasized the limitations of Christopher Robin's intellect, some readers may not notice that on this occasion he makes an important – and Platonically relevant – contribution. When Pooh asks him, 'What *is* the North Pole?'

> 'It's just a thing you discover,' said Christopher
> Robin carelessly, not being quite sure himself.

Probably most, even of dedicated Milnean Ursinologists, concentrate on the revelation of Christopher Robin's ignorance, and assume that this is just another example of Pooh as Socrates demonstrating his companion does not know what he is talking about.

This is true, but it is a trivial truth. The importance

of the passage lies in Christopher Robin's statement: the North Pole is something you *discover*. That is, it is something objectively existing, quite independently of any observer or discoverer.

This, of course, is precisely the view of mathematics which, to this day, is called Platonist, and contrasts with mathematical Conventionalism, which argues that it is simply the agreed rules that make mathematical statements true or false; and that these agreed rules might be changed.

Eeyore and the Platonic Forms

These examples do not exhaust the Platonic allusions in this chapter alone. Eeyore too has something valuable to say. We may note in passing that his ability to contribute shows what progress he has made since Chapter One: a tribute to Winnie-the-Pooh's tact and skill as a teacher as well as a philosopher.

Being Eeyore, he naturally wraps up his Platonic allusion in a complaint. As the explorers for the North Pole are lining up to start their march, Eeyore says, 'If I am the end of the Expo – what we're talking about – then let me *be* the end.' He complains that he keeps finding 'half a dozen of Rabbit's smaller friends-and-relations' behind him, so that 'this isn't an Expo – whatever it is – at all, it's simply a Confused Noise.' In this short passage, Eeyore refers to 'end', 'Expo – whatever it is', and 'Confused

Noise'. He clearly takes it for granted that each
of these expressions – 'end', 'Expotition', 'Confused
Noise' – has a right and proper meaning, and he is
complaining that the reality does not fit them.

Platonism is being carried a stage further, or
perhaps we should say that our understanding of it
is being widened. We have already seen Platonism
applied to mathematics. Now we see an example of
Plato's most characteristic doctrine, the very heart
of Platonism: his doctrine that all earthly things are
mere copies of eternal Forms or Ideas. Eeyore's complaint implies that there is a true Platonic Form or
Idea of an 'end', and we have no right to apply this
name to something that in no way conforms to that
Idea; that is not even a poor copy, but simply no
copy at all.

Allowing for some subtle differences, the same
applies to the other phrases. The first difference to
strike us is Eeyore's repeated inability to complete
the word 'Expotition'. Various interpretations may
come to our minds.

We may suppose that Eeyore, still at a very
early stage of his philosophic development, cannot
fully grasp either the word or the concept, or both,
though he is certain neither is a Confused Noise.

Or we may suppose that he is aware that 'Expotition' is not the normal form, and doubted whether
an abnormal word-form could relate to a Platonic
Form.

We must admit that 'Confused Noise' presents a different picture altogether, and one that introduces another aspect of Plato: his theory of how the universe began. For what is Eeyore's 'Confused Noise' but the primitive chaos that Plato's *Timaeus* describes as existing *before* the world came into existence?

In his own characteristic way, Eeyore is expressing the same horror of this primeval anarchy that we meet in Othello's 'Chaos is come again', in Milton's 'realm of Chaos and Old Night', and, perhaps less familiarly but with equal power, at the end of Pope's *Dunciad*:

> Lo! thy dread empire, Chaos! is restored;
> Light dies before thy uncreating word;
> Thy hand, great Anarch! lets the curtain fall,
> And universal Darkness buries All.

As Eeyore is the principal exponent of Plato in this section of the chapter, and as his tail is a recurrent theme in the whole work, we are not surprised to find him alluding to the Platonic Form of the tail.

The allusion is somewhat oblique, so we shall point it out. When little Roo fell into the river, Eeyore tried to rescue him by letting his own tail dangle in the river for Roo to catch hold of. He left his tail in the water long after – unknown to him – Roo had been rescued.

When at last he took his tail out, it was thoroughly

numb, and he grumbled about the widespread lack of understanding of tails and their dependent problems. 'A tail isn't a tail to *them*, it's just a Little Bit Extra at the back.' In other words, he is accusing the others of ignoring the Ideal Form of the Tail, and all that — if we dare say so — entails.

If anyone objects that this suggests Eeyore was getting obsessed with the Forms, the simple answer is that new students in any subject are often led to a somewhat excessive enthusiasm for some great genius in their field of study.

To Eeyore, whose world had hitherto been exceptionally narrow and earthbound, the discovery of the world of Ideal Forms must have been immensely exciting and liberating. If he became a little intoxicated, that is surely something for sympathetic understanding rather than criticism.

Pooh and the North Pole
Before we leave this chapter of *Winnie-the-Pooh*, we must return to our main hero. It was, after all, Pooh Bear himself who found the North Pole (that is, the ultimate constitution of the universe). That was only to be expected, but see how subtly Milne presents it.

While the others, like Eeyore (above), were making well-meant but futile attempts to rescue Roo, 'Pooh was getting something'. That something was a long pole, which he, helped by Kanga, used to get Roo out of the river. What follows?

> Christopher Robin . . . was looking at Pooh.
> 'Pooh,' he said, 'where did you find that pole?'
> Pooh looked at the pole in his hands.
> 'I just found it,' he said. 'I thought it ought to be useful. I just picked it up.'
> 'Pooh,' said Christopher Robin solemnly, 'the Expedition is over. You have found the North Pole!'

This passage is so rich in meanings that we must select only the most important.

First, consider how we meet the pole. Not as the object of the quest, but as a means of rescuing Roo. A superb, and all too rare, example of the combination of the philosophico-scientific search for truth with the ethical practice of caring for others.

Secondly, and closely linked with this, note the author's exquisite tact in making Kanga Pooh's partner in the rescue of her child.

Finally, observe the double meaning in Pooh's statement that he had 'just found' the P/pole. It alludes to the element of luck, of sheer serendipity, that has played a large part in many scientific discoveries. More importantly for Platonic implications, Pooh, like Plato, does not reveal his profoundest teachings to all and sundry. By now, surely all readers will recognize that his ignorance of the true nature of the pole is only apparent. But this time it is no mere assumption of Socratic ignorance. It is a cautious guarding of secrets too profound for those who have only started on the way.

Pooh and Plato's Banquet (the Symposium)

Many readers have commented on the emphasis on food in the World of Pooh; and not merely on food but on feasting. To Pooh and his friends, food is not just nutrition, not mere physical sustenance: it is, even on the superficial level, a giver of joy and, on some key occasions, of social warmth.

Once we are alerted to the Platonic riches of our text, we cannot fail to connect this aspect with Plato's *Symposium*. Christopher Robin's party at the end of *Winnie-the-Pooh* is the clearest parallel. Just as the drinking party Plato describes was given in honour of Agathon, because he had won the great drama competition, so our party was given in honour of Pooh Bear, because his courage and ingenuity had rescued Piglet from the flood.

The narrator's statement that 'they had all nearly eaten enough' echoes – more temperately – Plato's 'each man shall drink as much as he chooses'.

Love was the subject discussed at the Symposium. Winnie-the-Pooh was the subject discussed at Christopher Robin's party. We may notice right away that Socrates tells us that 'love has no parents', and we may remember that Pooh Bear seems equally to be parentless.

Thus prepared, we shall, as so often, look for many levels of meaning in Milne's multifaceted masterpiece. And this is all the more appropriate, as Plato, through the mouth of Socrates, emphasized many levels of love.

At the literal level, Pooh's rescue of Piglet showed love in a practical sense. But, just as Socrates showed love rising till it was refined into the rapt contemplation of abstract truth and beauty, so, we may be sure, the Great Bear's love of honey and 'little cake things with pink icing sugar' symbolizes his love of philosophic truth.

We have said enough to indicate the depth and breadth of Platonic scholarship in the *Pooh* texts. Now we turn to its equally rich treasures of Aristotelian philosophy.

Aristotle himself regarded logic as an essential philosopher's tool, and his own development of logic held the field for over two thousand years, until the birth of modern symbolic logic in the nineteenth century. Naturally, then, we expect to find reference to Aristotelian logic in Milne's masterpiece. And we are not disappointed. Look at the last paragraph of the following quotation.

Visiting Eeyore one day (WP, Ch. 4) Pooh notices something is missing.

> 'Why, what's happened to your tail?' he said
> in surprise.
>   'What *has* happened to it?' said Eeyore.
>   'It isn't there!'
>   'Are you sure?'
>   'Well, either a tail *is* there or it isn't there.
> You can't make a mistake about it.'

Now when Pooh Bear tells us that it is necessarily the case that Eeyore's tail is either there or not there and that there is no middle way, he is proclaiming one of the basic axioms of Aristotelian logic, the Law or Principle of the Excluded Middle.

We dealt with Aristotle's logic before touching on any other part of his philosophy because most philosophers, including Aristotle himself, regard logic as a necessary preliminary to philosophy. We now turn back to an earlier passage, which encapsulates two other key elements in Aristotelian philosophy. It all arises from Pooh's hearing some buzzing.

> 'If there's a buzzing-noise, somebody's making a buzzing-noise, and the only reason for making a buzzing-noise that *I* know of is because you're a bee.'

The first thing we notice is that Pooh assumes that the effect – buzzing – has a cause, something that makes it happen. This is precisely what Aristotle called an Efficient Cause ('efficient' here meaning 'having an effect'). Secondly, he concludes that in this instance, bees are the Efficient Cause of buzzing, because the buzzing is the effect of their action.

In passing, we note that he draws this conclusion from his knowledge of bees. This knowledge of the natural world, occurring at this particular moment, reminds us that Aristotle was a major biologist, as well as a major philosopher. We may point out too that when Aristotle erred in biology it was because he allowed abstract theory to take the place of concrete observation. An error that Pooh Bear never committed.

After further meditation on the buzzing, Pooh adds, 'And the only reason for being a bee that I know of is making honey . . . And the only reason for making honey is so as *I* can eat it.' In both these statements, Pooh assumes a reason, and reason here clearly means purpose. And the idea of purpose is fundamental to Aristotle's philosophy. In technical language, it was deeply teleological, and the purpose of an action was what he called its Final Cause (referring to the end or purpose for which it was done). Here Pooh gives us two examples of a Final Cause: the Final Cause of bees is to make honey; the Final Cause of honey is to feed Pooh.

So in a few short, clear and entertaining paragraphs, *Winnie-the-Pooh* gives us Aristotle's logic, two of his four Causes, and his basically teleological approach.

Pooh, Stoics and Epicureans

Though Plato and Aristotle remain the dominating figures in Greek philosophy, there were other important schools. These we must not neglect. Our author certainly did not. Most of us have at least heard the words 'Stoic' and 'Epicurean' or some of their derivatives. What do we find about them in *Pooh*?

In everyday use, stoicism means putting up uncomplainingly with suffering of any kind. As far as it goes, this is reasonably correct. Epictetus, perhaps the most famous of later Stoics, urged his hearers to attain an inner freedom that would make them happy in any circumstances. Both Pooh Bear himself and his companions illustrate this.

If we were asked which character in the World of Pooh is the greatest sufferer, all of us, I think, would plump for Eeyore. We first meet him thinking sadly. Though glad to see Pooh, he greets him 'in a gloomy manner'. At our next meeting, he is in the sad position of one whose birthday has been totally forgotten by all his friends. Yet his bearing is truly Stoical, as well as stoical. When Pooh asks him what is the matter, he replies,

> 'Nothing, Pooh Bear, nothing. We can't all,
> and some of us don't. That's all there is to it.'
> 'Can't all *what*?' . . .
> 'Gaiety. Song-and-dance . . . Bon-hommy,'
> went on Eeyore gloomily. 'French word meaning bonhommy . . . I'm not complaining, but There It Is.'

Notice his clear statement that he is not complaining, which should exclude any misunderstanding, and his recognition of Things as They Are, another reference we must analyse in due course.

A few lines later, Eeyore asks, 'Why should I be sad? It's my birthday. The happiest day of the year.'

We must admit that soon after, his Stoicism nearly breaks down. He has returned Pooh's birthday wishes. Puzzled, Pooh points out that it is not *his* birthday. Eeyore explains:

> 'You don't always want to be miserable on
> my birthday, do you? . . . It's bad enough . . .
> being miserable myself, what with no presents
> and no cake and no candles, and no proper
> notice taken of me at all, but if everybody else
> is going to be miserable too –'

How are we to explain this? Simply by remembering that Eeyore is still at a very early stage of his philosopher's progress. Just as this explained – and excused – his obsession with Platonic Forms, it explains his occasional lapse from Stoic calm. Fortunately, we can show how much he had progressed by the time of *The House at Pooh Corner*.

There, when Roo and Piglet are playing Poohsticks, they see Eeyore, who has fallen into the water, floating by, 'looking very calm, very digni-

---

fied, with his legs in the air'. Not only does he look calm, but he comments on his friends' rather futile remarks with exactly that cool detachment that was the aim of Stoic philosophers.

Interesting though the Eeyore-related instances of Stoicism are, we naturally expect the deepest understanding and the most striking examples to come from Pooh Bear himself. Nor are we disappointed.

Between his first hearing the bees buzzing and his balloon flight, he climbs a tree in search of the honey. Unfortunately, when he has climbed quite high, a branch breaks under him and he falls to the ground. What does he do in these frightening and painful circumstances? Calmly, he analyses the situation.

'If only I hadn't –' he said, as he bounced

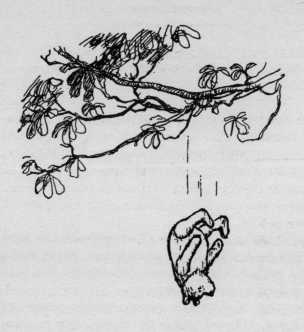

twenty feet on to the next branch.

'You see, what I *meant* to do,' he explained,
as he turned head-over-heels, and crashed on to
another branch thirty feet below, 'what I *meant*
to do –'

'Of course, it *was* rather –' he admitted, as
he slithered very quickly through the next six
branches.

'It all comes, I suppose,' he decided, as
he said good-bye to the last branch, spun

---

round three times, and flew gracefully into
a gorse-bush, 'it all comes of *liking* honey so
much.'

Where most people – even perhaps most philosophers – would have been reduced to inarticulate cries, or to articulate but regrettable language, Winnie-the-Pooh coolly considers the causes of his situation, examines his purpose (teleology again), and relates both to his own nature – a matter to which we must return.

Even at the bottom of his fall, always the most dangerous part, he is so relaxed that his descent into the gorse-bush is graceful.

What finer example of Stoic *ataraxia* ('untroubledness') could our author have given us within the limits of the kind of book he was writing? What may surprise some of our readers is to hear that it is an equally impressive example of Epicureanism. For while it is notorious that Epicurus taught that pleasure was the proper goal of life, people too often forget what sort of pleasure he recommended. In his own words, pleasure meant 'being neither pained in the body nor troubled in the soul'.

Obviously we cannot always avoid bodily pain, but the true Epicurean will always remain untroubled in soul. Epicurus himself, dying of dysentery and agonizing strangury, wrote to his friend of 'this happy day': happy because his physical pains were balanced 'by the joy in my soul as I recollect the conversations we have had together'. Thus the dead philosopher and the immortal Bear join hands across eighteen centuries.

The eminent Oxford philosopher Jonathan Barnes comments, 'the popular picture of a sybaritic Epicurean confronting a puritanical Stoic is a caricature: to an external observer there would be in truth little difference between members of the two sects.' All credit to Barnes for making the point, but Pooh Bear was there before him.

We have promised our readers to elaborate on another important aspect of Stoicism that has only been alluded to so far, and that in an oblique manner. This is the Stoic recommendation that one should live in accordance with nature. When Eeyore recognized that he lacked what he called 'bonhommy', he consoled himself by reflecting 'but There It Is'. Thus accepting the facts of his own nature. For we must remember that when the Stoics recommended us to live in accord with nature, they were not recommending a primitive, still less an animal kind of life. Each should live according to its *own* nature.

This is clearly what Eeyore meant by his 'There It Is'. It is also what Pooh himself meant by saying, 'It all comes of *liking* honey so much', as he is falling down the tree. That is, he explains his situation as a result of his nature. Note that, although he is in considerable discomfort and even danger, he does not complain of his nature or of the nature of the tree which has failed to support him.

Both Eeyore and Pooh Bear give us these clear and informative examples of the Stoic, but Tigger gives a better one still. They show the perfect Stoic who has reached the goal. Tigger shows the process of learning how to reach it. And this is both more informative and more encouraging to those of us who still have much progress to make.

The crucial passage is Chapter Two of *The House at Pooh Corner*, a chapter entitled 'Tigger Comes to the Forest and has Breakfast'. It is Tigger's breakfast that concerns us here. It is with reference to breakfast that our hospitable Bear asks, 'Do Tiggers like honey?'

'They like everything,' said Tigger cheerfully.

When, however, Tigger tasted honey, he quickly decided he did not like it. The most casual reader of *Winnie-the-Pooh* will remember that exactly the same process occurred with Piglet's haycorns and Eeyore's thistles. In each case, Tigger began by announcing that the particular food in question was what Tiggers liked best, and after experience, said that Tiggers did not like it. It was only when he tasted Roo's Extract of Malt that 'a peaceful smile came over his face as he said, "So *that's* what Tiggers like!"'

The passage – at the end of the chapter – continues:

> Which explains why he always lived at Kanga's
> house afterwards, and had Extract of Malt for
> breakfast, dinner, and tea.

In other words, having found what his nature was,
he proceeded to live in accordance with it.

We have now thoroughly demonstrated that a
proper reading of *Pooh* will leave us fully informed
of the breadth and depth of ancient classical philosophy. It would be easy enough to reveal the
wealth of neo-Platonic and medieval philosophy in
the same work, but it would be rather too technical
and specialized for this elementary introduction. So
we pass on to that group generally classified as the
Rationalist philosophers of the seventeenth century:
Descartes, Leibniz and Spinoza. Their contemporary
Hobbes, who has always refused to fit neatly into any
category, will come at the end of the next chapter, as
a bridge between the Rationalists and the Empiricists.

3

Pooh and the seventeenth-century Rationalists

The description 'seventeenth-century Rationalist' is usually applied to Descartes (1596–1650), Spinoza (1632–77) and Leibniz (1646–1716). Though there were vast differences between their philosophies, they shared a confidence in the power of reason alone to discover the nature of the universe; hence their name. They also shared the closely related belief that in principle everything could be explained. Readers will naturally expect to find these views illustrated and criticized in the two *Pooh* books, and they will not be disappointed.

We look first for an example of the typically Rationalist *a priori* method. That is, arguing from first principles instead of from knowledge gained by experience (for which see Chapters Four and Five).

The example I have chosen is the episode of Pooh's search for honey. We have already seen that this displayed his profound knowledge of Aristotle. Equally, it shows he knew all about the Rationalist claim to know the world by sheer force of reason. When he says, 'And the only reason for being a bee that I know of is making honey', he powerfully expresses the view that reason alone can give him an adequate knowledge of the nature of bees. This brilliant example of the *a priori* apiarist sums up the Rationalist position in one short and memorable sentence.

So much for Pooh Bear's illustration of Rationalism. Now for his criticism. A few pages later, he tells Christopher Robin, 'You never can tell with bees.' This doubt clearly undermines the confident claim to understand bees by reason alone. Pooh's previous statement remains a brilliant statement of a basic Rationalist principle, but it also subjects that principle to a radical criticism.

A moment's reflection shows that this criticism goes further still. Most obviously, it shows the limitations of unaided reason. But the word 'never' also denies the other great Rationalist belief: the belief that everything could be explained.

When we turn to the particular theories of the major Rationalists, we find a wealth of detailed evidence that Milne knew Descartes, Spinoza and Leibniz as thoroughly as he knew Plato and Aristotle.

Descartes

Descartes' search for a proposition that could not possibly be doubted led him eventually to his famous 'I think, therefore I am'. Several modern philosophers have argued that Descartes took the meaning of 'I' for granted, whereas in fact it is highly complex; and that all he was really justified in saying was that thinking was going on. Nowhere is this problem presented more vividly than in *Winnie-the-Pooh*, Chapter Two, 'Pooh Goes Visiting and Gets Into a Tight Place'.

When Pooh arrives at Rabbit's, he asks, 'Is anybody at home?' There is no answer, so he repeats his question. This time there is an answer.

> 'No!' said a voice; and then added, 'You needn't shout so loud. I heard you quite well the first time.'
> 'Bother!' said Pooh. 'Isn't there anybody here at all?'
> 'Nobody.'

After pondering the situation, Pooh thinks to himself, 'There must be somebody there, because somebody must have *said* "Nobody." ' So he put his head back in the hole, and said,

> 'Hallo, Rabbit, isn't that you?'

———

'No,' said Rabbit, in a different voice this time.

Further dialogue elicits the statement that Rabbit has gone to visit Pooh Bear. To which Pooh answers, 'But this *is* Me!'

'What sort of Me?'
'Pooh Bear.'
'Are you sure?' . . .
'Quite, quite sure,' said Pooh.

Once we are thinking about Descartes, there is no difficulty in seeing that this situation and the dialogue arising from it simply dramatize the problematical nature of that apparently simple word 'I'.

First, was Pooh correct in deducing the presence of somebody from the fact of hearing a voice saying there was nobody there? If he was, what sort of somebody would call itself nobody? Have we got here a somebody that is not an 'I' to itself? And what light – or perhaps what darkness – does this throw on the whole problem that Descartes so casually glossed over?

To make quite sure that we know what philosophical problem is being discussed, Milne goes on to put it in the plainest terms when he makes Rabbit answer Pooh's statement that he is 'Me' with the question 'What sort of Me?' One would suppose that even the most casual reader could hardly fail to see the significance of this question. Yet, to the shame of modern philosophers, it has passed unnoticed.

They have been equally blind to the obvious Cartesian references in the sections that deal with Christopher Robin's education. Doubtless all our readers are familiar with Chapter Five of *The House at Pooh Corner*, entitled 'In Which Rabbit Has a Busy Day, and We Learn What Christopher Robin Does in the Mornings'. It is Eeyore who tells Rabbit and Piglet – and us:

'What does Christopher Robin do in the mornings? He learns. He becomes Educated.'

The last chapter confirms this by describing Christopher Robin unloading his newly acquired knowledge on Winnie-the-Pooh. He tells him about Kings and Queens, Factors, Europe, Suction Pumps, Knights, and the products of Brazil. In passing, we may notice that his pride in communicating a collection of unrelated facts is typical of the half-educated. More to our present purpose is the contrast with Pooh Bear.

It is clear that he has had no formal education. It is also clear that, as we have abundantly proved and shall prove even more abundantly, he has a profound knowledge and understanding of all philosophy. Thinking Cartesianly, we cannot fail to recognize a clear example of Descartes' belief in innate ideas: ideas with which we are born, and which, as the *Pan Dictionary of Philosophy* puts it, 'may be captured by the method of reason'. Where Christopher Robin had to plod wearily through the accumulation of trivial facts, Pooh Bear was familiar with the most complex ideas of the greatest philosophers simply by using his reason to consider the ideas he was born with.

Finally, the whole book is an overwhelming refutation of Descartes' notorious theory that all animals are mere automata. Pooh Bear, Piglet, Kanga and Wol automata? One has only to ask the question to see its utter absurdity. Even the Smallest of Rabbit's friends-and-relations to take part in the Expotition to the North Pole is a full and distinct person, with a specific philosophical reference. We read –

And the last and smallest friend-and-relation
was so upset to find the whole Expotition
was saying 'Hush!' to *him*, that he
buried himself head downwards in a
crack in the ground, and stayed there
for two days until the danger was
over, and then went home in a great
hurry, and lived quietly with his Aunt
ever-afterwards. His name was Alexander Beetle.

It is another disgraceful example of careless reading
that no one has yet commented on the significance
of the name 'Alexander' in combination with its
bearer's behaviour. The reference is obviously to
the eminent realist philosopher, Samuel Alexander
(1859–1938). Two of Alexander's outstanding charac-
teristics were his proclaimed dislike of argument and
his insistence that the world existed independently of
any observing mind. His little namesake effectively
demonstrated the first by refusing to argue with those
who told him to hush, while his use of a crack in
the ground demonstrates the independent reality of
the material world. Thus even this – in every sense –
minor character refutes two key Cartesian doctrines:
the doctrine that animals are automata, and the
doctrine that only the existence of an undeceptive
Creator can justify our confidence in the existence
of the world.

A shallow critic might say we are forgetting the

---

nature of a fable, which is precisely to treat animals
as human, without at all implying they have anything
like a human nature. This ignores the fact that an
author as wise as ours does nothing without deep
consideration. His every word is full of meaning.
He chose to use animals because he wanted to say
something about animals. And one thing he wanted
to say was that they are not automata.

Spinoza

At this stage, some readers may be asking impatiently, 'When are we going to hear about a character
who quite obviously represents the Rationalist attitude to life and its problems?' Without delay then,
we come to Rabbit's

PLAN TO CAPTURE BABY ROO

1. *General Remarks.* Kanga runs faster than any
   of Us, even Me.
2. *More General Remarks.* Kanga never takes her
   eyes off Baby Roo, except when he's safely
   buttoned up in her pocket.
3. *Therefore.* If we are to capture Baby Roo, we must
   get a Long Start, because Kanga runs faster than
   any of Us, even Me. (*See* 1.)
4. *A Thought.* If Roo had jumped out of Kanga's
   pocket and Piglet had jumped in, Kanga
   wouldn't know the difference, because Piglet
   is a Very Small Animal.

5. Like Roo.
6. But Kanga would have to be looking the other way first, so as not to see Piglet jumping in.
7. See 2.
8. *Another Thought.* But if Pooh was talking to her very excitedly, she *might* look the other way for a moment.
9. And then I could run away with Roo.
10. Quickly.
11. *And Kanga wouldn't discover the difference until Afterwards.*

What could remind us more forcibly of Spinoza's way of setting out his theories in numbered Propositions, Proofs and Corollaries? Rabbit is undoubtedly the Spinoza of the World of Pooh – though of course that is far from being his only function.

This example is unusual because it illustrates the style rather than the content of the philosopher in question. But there is no lack of reference to Spinoza's thought. Here too we find Rabbit playing a vital part. If we think back to the conversation between him and Pooh Bear (WP, Ch. 2), we remember that it raised the question, Have we got here a somebody who is not an 'I' to itself? Looking at this question through Spinozan lenses – an appropriate metaphor as Spinoza made his living by grinding lenses – we remember at once that Roger Scruton tells us that Spinoza does not see life from the point of view of an 'I'.

Professor Scruton was speaking of Spinoza's moral

philosophy, and there is another dramatic illustration of this at the end of Winnie-the-Pooh's visit. He has enjoyed Rabbit's hospitality so fully that he gets stuck in the doorway. A clear example of Spinoza's comment on the consequences of taking pleasure as a goal: 'After that enjoyment follows pain.' As in several other instances, Pooh Bear nobly sacrifices his own comfort and even his dignity to provide a striking lesson in moral philosophy.

I fear I must disappoint readers who were looking forward eagerly to a discussion of Spinoza's pantheism. Pooh and theology, even natural theology, must wait for another volume. This limitation will apply also to our next subject: Leibniz.

Leibniz

'Tigger is all right, *really*,' said Piglet lazily.
'Of course he is,' said Christopher Robin.
'Everybody is *really*,' said Pooh. 'That's what *I* think,' said Pooh. 'But I don't suppose I'm right,' he said.
'Of course you are,' said Christopher Robin.

This short dialogue encapsulates the popular picture of the philosophy of Leibniz. Leibniz is usually associated with the doctrine summed up by Voltaire that 'this is the best of all possible worlds' – on which

F. H. Bradley commented 'and everything in it is a necessary evil' – a more sardonic version of Pooh's casually worded but significant disclaimer.

We may note in passing that Milne summed up in five lines what it took Voltaire a whole book to say. It would be rash, though, to suppose that Milne dismissed quite so cavalierly a philosopher whom Bertrand Russell described as 'one of the supreme intellects of all time'. And in fact we find more material on Leibniz that displays the mixture of profundity and concision we have learned to expect in Milne's great work.

Staying briefly with the popular picture of Leibniz, we should look more carefully at the implications of the phrase 'possible worlds'. Though this was the best of all *possible* worlds, in Leibniz's view, God could have made other worlds, and these would have had other creatures in them. What else can we understand by Pooh Bear's hunt for the Woozle? Undoubtedly the Woozle was one of these creatures that might have existed in some possible but not actual world. The more ambiguous ontological status of the Heffalump is something we shall examine in Chapter Four.

Now let us, yet once more, look back at Pooh Bear's assertions, that 'the only reason for making a buzzing-noise that *I* know of is because you're a bee . . . And the only reason for being a bee that I know of is making honey.'

As well as clearly referring to Aristotelian teleology and the Rationalist confidence in *a priori* knowledge, this refers just as clearly to one of Leibniz's basic principles: 'the principle that a reason must be given ... or, in the common phrase, that nothing happens without a cause' (usually called the Principle of Sufficient Reason).

Equally important in his system was the Principle of Contradiction. Again, Winnie-the-Pooh's demonstration of this with relation to Aristotelian logic applies just as well to Leibniz.

Some merely literary critics of the more traditional sort have complained that the characters in *Pooh* books are confined to very limited and repetitive roles. Eeyore is always self-pitying, Tigger always bouncy, Owl emptily verbose, Rabbit bureaucratically domineering. Winnie-the-Pooh himself, they say, is eternally thinking of 'a little something' involving honey.

Even on their own elementary level, this shows grossly careless reading. From our more elevated philosophical standpoint, it shows them totally blind to the obvious fact that, so far as their complaint has some factual basis, this basis provides a simple model of Leibniz's theory of Identity in Individuals.

Leibniz posed the problem of how he could know that, if he spent some time in Paris and then moved to Germany, the 'me' he was aware of was the same person in both places. He admitted the obvious answer: that consulting his own memory would tell him. But that was an *a posteriori* proof. (One based on experience.) As a Rationalist, he insisted, there must also be some *a priori* reason. (Here, one based on innate first principles.)

He argued that in every true proposition everything that can be said about the subject is contained in the notion of the subject. So that a full knowledge of any individual would enable us to know everything about that individual's past, present and future. This, at first sight, is a staggering suggestion, and Leibniz admitted that such complete knowledge belonged only to God.

With this in mind, we can see that the consistent behaviour some have criticized is Milne's way of making Leibniz's theory easy to understand. He shows us that certain kinds of behaviour belong to the very essence of his characters. Thus he gives glimpses of the God's-eye view that Leibnitz talks about.

Any attempt to reach a God's-eye view is precisely what our next philosopher would have rejected.

A note on Thomas Hobbes (1588–1679)

It is difficult to fit Hobbes into our scheme, and this is typical of him. Just as in his own day while parliamentarians condemned him as an advocate of absolute monarchy, monarchists condemned him as an apologist for Cromwell, so we find it hard to classify him in philosophical terms.

The second sentence of his most famous work, *Leviathan*, is: 'The Original of them all [the Thoughts of man] is that which we call SENSE. (For there is no conception in a man's mind, which hath not at first, totally, or by parts, been begotten upon the organs of Sense.)' Here Hobbes seems to suggest a strictly empirical approach, basing all knowledge on the experience we gain from the use of our senses. This, of course, would place Hobbes in diametrical opposition to the Rationalist philosophers. The historical fact that one of Hobbes's first philosophical writings was a set of objections to Descartes' *Meditations* seems therefore to have a symbolical significance.

On the other hand though, no one was more passionately devoted to the essentially Rationalist discipline of geometry than Hobbes. It was the accidental reading of the theorem of Pythagoras that awakened his intellect. He called geometry 'the onely science it hath pleased God hitherto to bestow on mankind'. Over and over again, he emphasizes that clear definitions, as in geometry, are essential to clear thought.

Yet on all his efforts at transparent clarity the final judgment must be that of the eminent seventeenth-century historian D. H. Pennington, who wrote 'Commentators on the whole agree in praising the logical and uncompromising clarity of his argument and go on to differ fundamentally about what he meant.'

Leviathan is primarily a work of political philosophy, and its essential argument is that the natural state of humanity 'is a condition of Warre of every one against every one', in which our life is 'solitary, poore, nasty, brutish, and short'. The whole World of Pooh is a decisive refutation of this thesis.

Right at the beginning, we have Christopher Robin helping Winnie-the-Pooh in his quest for honey. Both co-operate in the rescue of Piglet, when he is cut off by a flood. Owl is always ready to advise; Rabbit to organize. Owl's advice may be impracticable; Rabbit's organization bossy and futile; but there is no doubt of their goodwill. When one of the least of Rabbit's numerous friends-and-relations is missing, there is an immediate and active response to the call for a search. On a still larger scale, the Expotition to the North Pole and the party that ends *Winnie-the-Pooh* show us all the inhabitants of the World of Pooh joining together for adventure or festivity. And these are but a few examples.

Moreover, this peaceful and happy condition is not created by any kind of government. It has no state, no police, no laws or punishments. Again, a flat denial of Hobbes, who argued that only an absolute despot could control the mutually destructive urges of human beings.

4

Pooh and the British Empiricist tradition

Empiricism is usually defined as the doctrine that all knowledge is derived from experience, whether that experience is the sort common to all of us or the specialized kind generally called science. As John Locke, the founder of the school, put it, 'No man's knowledge can go beyond his experience.' This doctrine has been particularly strong in England.

John Locke (1632–1704)

Just as mathematics was the model for the Rationalists we considered in the last chapter, so the physical sciences were the model for the Empiricists. Indeed, in his introductory 'Epistle to the Reader' (of *An Essay* on the Human Understanding), Locke says his ambition was merely to be employed 'as an under-labourer in clearing the ground a little' for such scientists as 'the incomparable Mr Newton'. And it is especially in the area of experience and experiment that we find the Great Bear demonstrating his deep knowledge of Empiricism.

While bearing in mind the warning we have given against assuming that Winnie-the-Pooh necessarily holds a view just because he expounds it with unparalleled clarity, it does seem reasonable to say that he is at the opposite pole from the aerated sort of philosophy recommended by Colin McGinn, who wrote, 'the philosopher wishes to know, without being roused from his armchair, what is *essential* to the various mental phenomena.' It seems fair to suppose that the Great Bear would have considered the concept of essential mental phenomena, divorced from the outside world, at best vacuous, at worst seriously misleading.

Pooh and the Jar of HUNNY

However anxious we may be to avoid the charge of ethnocentrism, we can hardly deny that Winnie-the-Pooh is a very English bear. It is therefore natural to find him, in every sense, a stout supporter of the British Empiricist tradition, which maintains that all statements must be testable by experience. Here we have an excellent example of the empirical approach in his investigation and final confirmation of the hypothesis that the honey jar did in fact contain honey and nothing else.

As soon as he got home, he went to the larder; and he stood on a chair, and took down a very large jar of honey from the top shelf. It had HUNNY written on it, but, just to make sure, he took off the paper cover and looked at it, and it *looked* just like honey. 'But you never can tell,' said Pooh. 'I remember my uncle saying once that he had seen cheese just this colour.' So he put his tongue in, and took a large lick. 'Yes,' he said, 'it is. No doubt about that. And honey, I should say, right down to the bottom of the jar. Unless, of course,' he said, 'somebody put

cheese in at the bottom just for a joke. Perhaps I
had better go a *little* further . . . just in case . . .
Ah!' And he gave a deep sigh. 'I *was* right. It *is*
honey, right the way down.'

Note the cautious steps by which he established
his conclusion. First he went to the shelf where –
as we know from other evidence – he kept honey.
Thus there was already some degree of probability
that a jar there would be a jar of honey. But, to a
philosophical mind, it was a very moderate degree
of probability. It might *have been* a jar of honey, but
now an empty one, or one refilled with some other
substance. It might never have been a honey jar at
all, but one that looked so like a honey jar that Pooh
had put it on his honey shelf by mistake.

At a later stage of our history, one might suppose
that Kanga had taken it upon herself to tidy Pooh's
dwelling – just as she tried to do later with Wol's
dwelling – and had put a non-honey jar on the
honey-jar shelf. We must, I think, dismiss this
explanation, because Kanga and Roo did not come
to the forest till well after the great honey jar experiment. Leaving other possible explanations aside, we
return to Pooh's investigation.

Having taken the jar from the shelf, Pooh looks
at the label. 'HUNNY' it says. We must not allow
ourselves to be distracted by the somewhat unusual
form of the word. Though a philosopher, Pooh was

not a pedant, and was moreover the founder of the concept of Wobbly Spelling. His concern here was not orthographic convention but the relation of word to referent. In other words, did the contents of the jar match the name on the outside?

He took off the cover and looked inside. It looked like honey all right, but Pooh could not be satisfied by such superficial evidence. Like every philosopher, he knew that appearances can be deceptive. So next he tastes. Taste confirms sight and label. And we must remember that nobody could claim more expert knowledge of the taste – and texture – of honey than Winnie-the-Pooh.

The critical reader may object that the substance might look and taste exactly like honey, and yet be different in ways that, say, chemical analysis would reveal. I think we may dismiss this as intuitively implausible. The World of Pooh is not the world of science fiction nor is it a world containing food technologists.

Note also that Pooh constantly exposes his hypothesis to disconfirmation. Any one of his tests might have destroyed it. That is, he consistently fulfilled Sir Karl Popper's requirement: *'the criterion of the scientific status of a theory is its falsifiability, or refutability, or testability'* (his emphasis).

Now let us go on to examine the whole chapter of

which the HUNNY incident is only a part: that is, Chapter Five, 'In Which Piglet meets a Heffalump'.

Christopher Robin begins by announcing that he has seen a Heffalump. Piglet comments that he saw one once, but adds, 'At least, I think I did. Only perhaps it wasn't.'

Then comes the first really important contribution, naturally from Winnie-the-Pooh. ' "So did I," said Pooh, wondering what a Heffalump was like.'

Our first response is to ask what *exactly* did Pooh's utterance refer to. Hasty readers may jump – all too many, we fear, have jumped – to the conclusion that he was merely joining in the general claim to have seen a Heffalump. This interpretation is obviously absurd, being blatantly inconsistent with his wondering what a Heffalump was like. Such an interpretation would imply that Pooh was uttering a statement that was either meaningless or false. (If he did not know what a Heffalump was like, he could not truthfully claim he had seen one.) As both of these are obviously incompatible with what we know of Pooh, we must look further.

We need not look far. The answer lies in the uncertain nature of Piglet's statement. We may break this down into three propositions:

1. He once saw a Heffalump.
2. He thinks he once saw a Heffalump.
3. Perhaps what he saw was not a Heffalump.

It is to the united effect of all three that Pooh is responding. He is in fact performing a thought experiment, by imagining that he too has had an experience that *might* have been the experience of seeing a Heffalump, but also might not have been. In such a situation, he would naturally wonder what a Heffalump was like. If you are not sure what a Heffalump is like, it follows that you cannot be sure whether you have seen one.

As Piglet and Pooh went home together after this conversation, they 'helped each other across the stepping stones, and . . . began to talk in a friendly way about this and that, and Piglet said, "If you see what I mean, Pooh," and Pooh said, "It's just what I think myself, Piglet." '

Milne has chosen not to enlighten us on the subject of their conversation, probably because he did not wish to distract us from the main thrust of his argument by introducing an irrelevant topic. He does however introduce us to Winnie-the-Pooh's way of teaching – his pedagogic methodology, to use a phrase more familiar to some of our readers.

As we shall see more and more clearly as this chapter goes on, Pooh is here adopting the experienced teacher's well-known method of encouraging pupils to participate actively in the learning process, to make their own discoveries, even to let them suppose they are teaching the teacher. The reference to helping each other across the stepping stones is clearly a metaphor for such mutual aid in solving intellectual problems, while the ensuing dialogue hints strongly that these problems were precisely philosophical.

Then, as they came to the Six Pine Trees, Pooh made his momentous announcement. 'I have decided to catch a Heffalump.'

In other words, he is going to clarify Piglet's mind on the subject of Heffalumps.

Having stated his intention, Pooh continues to encourage Piglet to ask questions and make suggestions. First he builds up Piglet's confidence by telling him that it must be a Cunning Trap, *'so you will have to help me, Piglet'* (my emphasis).

His positive proposals seem a little odd, even naive. To dig a deep pit – however enlarged by being called a Deep Pit – and expect that a Heffalump would fall into it unawares, whether because he was looking up to see if it was going to rain or because he was looking up to see if it was going to stop raining, does seem impractical. We fear this is just another of those places where the rashly critical readers, whom we have so often had cause to rebuke, will again open their mouths only to insert their clod-hopping great boots.

The wiser will wait and suspend judgment. They will be encouraged by Pooh's 'that's why Heffalumps hardly *ever* get caught'.

Before the next stage in the experiment, Pooh

makes an interesting, though almost parenthetical (internal) comment: 'he felt sure that a Very Clever Brain could catch a Heffalump'. With the usual cautions against taking any one statement by or about Winnie-the-Pooh as definitive, this does suggest a strongly materialist position, perhaps of the sort later elaborated by Patricia Smith Churchland in her brilliant *Neurophilosophy: Toward a Unified Science of the Mind-Brain.*

When he goes on to ask Piglet what bait Piglet would use to catch Pooh, Piglet, like the conscientious but rather plodding pupil he is, answers that he would use honey.

Then, of course, comes the brilliant application of empirical principles to the jar of HUNNY, which we have already examined. The next few steps may be summarized briefly. Pooh brings the honey –

somewhat reduced by his conscientious experiment.
Piglet puts it at the bottom of the pit, and they return
to their respective homes.

Both have bad nights. It is hunger that disturbs
Pooh, and finally drives him to the pit, where his
attempt to eat the last of the honey leaves his head
stuck in the pot. Nightmares about fierce and hostile
Heffalumps are the cause of Piglet's bad night. Here
we must pause for a moment to consider – one might
justly say – to savour the word Milne uses when
describing Piglet's state of mind: 'the word which
was *jigetting* about in his brain was "Heffalumps".'

'Jigetting'. Has any philosopher or any psychologist ever coined so superbly apt a word for the
state of mind in question? Ponder for a moment the

multiple meanings encapsulated in this single word. 'Jig' vividly suggests the dance of ideas in the uncontrolled sleeping mind. But 'jig' is also 'an appliance for guiding a tool' (*Chambers 20th Century Dictionary*). Perhaps therefore part of the brain's hardwiring; at least some sort of guide to thought processes. This suggestion of some fairly permanent guiding equipment is then undercut – by anyone familiar with William Empson's *Seven Types of Ambiguity* – by the latent hint of 'gadget', with its association of temporary, ad hoc makeshifts.

Piglet's anxious self-questionings on the subject of Heffalumps reveal the effects of his long association with the Great Bear. Notice how systematically he moves from the most general question ('What was a Heffalump like?') to questions about its attributes ('*Did* it come when you whistled? And *how* did it come?'), then to questions about the Heffalump's characteristic behaviour to Pigs as such, then to particular sorts of Pig, finally narrowing the focus to speculating on a Heffalump's behaviour to a Pig who had a grandfather called TRESPASSERS WILLIAM.

Unable to answer these questions, he decides to go to the Deep Pit and see whether a Heffalump is trapped in it. Notice how the McGinn type of armchair – or in-bed – philosophy proves empty in spite of its formal elegance, and only on-the-spot inspection will bring real answers. Even Piglet realizes this.

What he sees, of course, is Pooh with his head stuck in the jar. Terrified by this apparition, Piglet flees to Christopher Robin. Together they discover the truth.

Piglet's embarrassment at his folly is so acute that he runs home and retires to bed with a headache. Sorry though one feels for him, his response does corroborate the suspicion that his nature is too sensitive to bear the disappointments that must inevitably occur in the life of an experimentalist. Observe the contrast with Pooh. He went off to breakfast with Christopher Robin; and when Christopher Robin said, ' "Oh, Bear! How I do love you!" "So do I," said Pooh.'

His reply, which is given special emphasis by being the end of the chapter, tells us that he is well satisfied with the result of the Heffalump experiment.

This perhaps calls for explanation. After all, some may object, the aim of the Plan was to catch a Heffalump. It not only singularly failed to do that, it first terrified and then embarrassed Piglet, and exposed Pooh himself to discomfort and ridicule. The whole thing was a fiasco.

By this time, we hope our more cautious readers have learnt that it is always wiser to assume that Winnie-the-Pooh knew what he was doing. Far from being a failure, the episode of the Heffalump Trap was a triumphant success, teaching at least three valuable lessons:

73

1. Readers who are alert as well as cautious will have
noticed a vital early warning. During the discussion
on Heffalumps that opens the chapter, Christopher
Robin remarks that one does not often see them.
What follows?

'Not now,' said Piglet.
'Not at this time of year,' said Pooh.

If only Piglet had realized the full meaning of what
he said, and had remembered it, what a lot of trouble
he would have saved himself! If the Heffalump is
rarely seen now, trying to catch one without reliable
information about its habitat is, to put it mildly, a very
dubious enterprise. It is even more dubious if you are
so vague about its appearance that you are not sure
whether you have seen one or not.

Pooh, of course, did his best to reinforce Piglet's
all too fleeting intuition of the truth by his addition.
'Not at this time of year' says in the clearest possible
way that expecting even to *see* a Heffalump is an
unseasonable hope. Unseasonable: unreasonable.

Their pleasant philosophical conversation on the
way home had clearly raised Pooh's hopes that his
little pupil had made such progress that he would
rise to the occasion when his teacher put him to the
test by saying he had decided to catch a Heffalump.

Even without any further guidance, we should see
that he hoped Piglet would, however respectfully,

cast doubt on so dubious a project. But this is so important a crux that our author lays the information plainly before us. The passage continues:

> Pooh nodded his head several times as he
> said this, and waited for Piglet to say 'How?'
> or 'Pooh, you couldn't!' or something helpful
> of that sort, but Piglet said nothing.

There we have it. We are explicitly told that Pooh hoped for a sceptical 'How?' or a refuting 'You couldn't!' All he got was silence. For the sake of his feelings as a teacher, it is as well he did not know, as we do, that Piglet was silent because, taking this wildly unrealistic project seriously, he was disappointed that he had not proposed it himself. Pooh quickly realized that the only hope of bringing Piglet to understand the absurdity of the plan was to carry it out in detail.

We commented earlier that Pooh's suggestions about the operation of the Heffalump Trap seemed a little odd. At that stage we asked our readers to suspend judgment. Now all is clear. In the light of our recent analysis, it is obvious that Pooh was not trying to construct a real trap for a real Heffalump, but simply parodying the process of setting up experimental apparatus in the – by now, fading – hope that Piglet would notice the absurdity of the means and so be led to see the unreality of the end.

Like many another good teacher, he overrated his pupil's intelligence and had to carry the process of disillusioning him much further than he had originally expected. Success did come in the end. Piglet realized his folly. At the very least, we can be fairly confident that he will not try again to trap a Heffalump. With rather less confidence, we may hope he will not embark on any project without a clearer picture of ends and means.

2. This indicates the second valuable lesson to be learnt from this episode. It is a convincing example of the important truth that no experiment can be a total failure. When we talk of a failed experiment, we usually mean one that did not confirm the hypothesis we were hopefully testing. But 'failure' in this sense teaches us that there was some shortcoming either in the hypothesis or in the experiment itself. However disappointed we may be, we should be able to profit from our experience, just as Piglet, we hope, profited from his. This is plain enough. The next lesson is more complex.

3. So far, we have been assuming that the Heffalump was a real, physical being, that could, in principle, be caught in some sort of trap. We must now ask whether this assumption is correct. What do we found it on?

The only evidence for the real existence of the

Heffalump is contained in three statements at the beginning of Chapter Five:

1. Christopher Robin said he had seen a Heffalump that day.
2. Piglet said he had seen one once.
3. Pooh Bear said he had seen one.

At first we are likely to be convinced by the converging evidence of several apparently independent witnesses. All the more when those witnesses number three. However rational we like to picture ourselves, the ancient belief that three is a mystical number probably lurks somewhere in the murkier depths of our minds. 'What I tell you three times is true,' said the Bellman in *The Hunting of the Snark*, and when a triple repetition has separate sources, this gives a rational colour to our credulity.

Nevertheless, credulity it is, as we shall immediately demonstrate. First, are these three witnesses genuinely independent? Careful examination of the text makes it clear they are not. Piglet is, we know from other evidence, highly suggestible, especially when the suggestion comes from Christopher Robin, whom he regards with somewhat exaggerated respect. Here he is obviously following Christopher Robin's lead. And, as we have already shown, following it in a very hesitant and dubious manner. Similarly, we have shown that Pooh's statement is simply a thought experiment, without necessary reference to anything in the real world.

This leaves us with the solitary and unsupported statement by Christopher Robin. As this is the sole evidence we have of the sighting of a Heffalump, we must examine it with the greatest care. What is the context in which Christopher Robin makes this key statement? When he, Pooh and Piglet 'were all talking together'. Here surely we have a situation in which people are often more concerned to impress their companions than to exemplify scientific accuracy.

This admittedly is speculative, but there is corroboration from the author's next piece of information. He tells us that Christopher Robin spoke when he had 'finished the mouthful he was eating'. Whatever his intellectual failings, Christopher Robin had been properly brought up, and would not speak with his mouth full. True, he did speak 'with his mouth full' on the Expotition to the North Pole, but then he was obviously in the role of hardened explorer, free from the civilized conventions that bound him on his own territory. But in the context of the Heffalump discussion, while he was eating, others could hold the floor. He therefore had a special need to regain the conversational initiative. How better could he do this than by saying he had just had a remarkable personal experience?

There may still be those who remained unconvinced, but even the most obstinate sceptic must admit the devastating force of the adverb Milne uses to modify Christopher Robin's statement: 'carelessly'. He 'said *carelessly*: "I saw a Heffalump today, Piglet." ' (My emphasis.) In view of what we have shown about Piglet's suggestibility, we can understand why Christopher Robin addressed him by name.

In this context, there is no doubt that 'carelessly' applies not only to the manner but, and more importantly, to the matter of Christopher Robin's assertion. Milne gives us clear warning not to take it at face value.

Now that we understand the context, the rest follows easily enough. We can evaluate and dismiss a tempting but fallacious interpretation. Some Pooh scholars have invoked the concept of WS (Wobbly Spelling) to suggest that 'Heffalump' is a WS variant of 'Elephant'. These scholars support this improbable hypothesis by pointing to the illustrations that show elephants above both Pooh and Piglet while they are dreaming of Heffalumps.

Now WS does play a vital role in certain sections of the *Pooh* books, but here it is totally irrelevant, for reasons which we shall demonstrate.

1.   The concept of Wobbly Spelling by definition applies only to the written word. There is no justification for transferring it to the spoken word.

2. Though Christopher Robin says little about the Heffalump he claims to have seen, he does give us one detail that effectively destroys the elephant hypothesis. He says it was 'just *lumping* along' (my emphasis). Now the elephant, in spite of its size, is remarkable for the delicacy of its tread. It used to be – perhaps still is – a high compliment to a Thai lady to tell her that she walked like an elephant. Whatever Christopher Robin described, it cannot have been an elephant.

3. The problem of E. H. Shepard's two elephant pictures is more subtle. To argue that it is illegitimate to interpret a philosophical text by its illustrations is a tempting line of argument, but one we should resist in this case. Shepard's illustrations are too integral to the text to be so cavalierly dismissed. If Shepard depicted Pooh and Piglet dreaming of elephants when they thought they were dreaming of Heffalumps, he had good reason for doing so. The reason was to illustrate the thought of one of the great names in British Empirical philosophy.

We are, of course, talking about Bishop Berkeley.

Bishop Berkeley (1685–1753)

Berkeley was an Empiricist with a difference. Whereas Locke argued that all our knowledge came from experience or reflection on experience, and that experience was experience of the outside world, Berkeley argued that the only experience we could be sure of was experience of ideas in our minds. All we could 'know' of the outside world was our own perceptions of it. In an often quoted phrase, he said, 'to be is to be perceived'. It would be wise to remember that the whole phrase ran, 'To be is to be perceived or to perceive' (*'Esse est aut percipi aut percipere'* in Berkeley's original Latin).

This theory raised an obvious problem about the status of physical objects when nobody was there to perceive them. Did a table in an empty room disappear, only to reappear the moment somebody came in? This was unconvincing – intuitively implausible, to use the professional jargon. On the other hand, if it continued to exist when there was nobody there to perceive it, didn't that destroy Berkeley's whole philosophy?

Berkeley himself had no difficulty with this problem. He was a bishop, and in those days bishops generally believed in God. So even when there was no other perceiver, objects continued to exist because God was everywhere and all-perceiving. The problem and the Berkeleyan solution are neatly summed up in a pair of limericks. The first was composed by Ronald Knox, wit, priest, detective-story writer and translator of the Bible. He wrote,

There was once a young man who said, 'God
Must think it exceedingly odd
  If he finds that this tree
  Continues to be
When there's no one about in the Quad.'

An anonymous answer ran:

Dear Sir, Your astonishment's odd:
I am always about in the Quad,
  And that's why the tree
  Will continue to be,
Since observed by Yours faithfully, God.

With Berkeley in mind, let us return to the question, Why did Shepard picture Piglet and Pooh dreaming of elephants instead of Heffalumps? The answer is that he could not draw a Heffalump because he could not, even in imagination, perceive a Heffalump. Neither could Piglet or Pooh – nor could anybody else. And because no one can perceive a Heffalump, a Heffalump cannot exist.

Finally, a fourth interpretation. The Heffalump may be regarded as a symbol of philosophical truth: seldom seen, difficult to recognize, and 'hardly ever . . . caught'. Expecting to capture it at the bottom of a pit would then be an interesting variant on its traditional habitat at the bottom of a well.

This variation springs from no mere desire for novelty. Milne's metaphor adds another dimension, for it reminds us that the very search for truth may lead us into a trap. How many philosophers have derided their predecessors and their peers for precisely this reason.

One indeed, in a metaphor strikingly similar to the Heffalump Trap, said that the philosophical search for truth was like looking in a darkened room for a black cat, which was probably not there (F. H. Bradley, 1846–1924).

David Hume (1711–76)

In a more concrete way, few philosophers have criticized their fellows more devastatingly than our next subject. Indeed, perhaps his only rival as a destructive critic was one of his greatest admirers, Alfred Ayer (1910–89), who described Hume as 'to my mind the greatest of all British philosophers'.

It was Hume who, in a famous and often quoted statement, the very last paragraph of his *An Enquiry Concerning Human Understanding*, said,

> If we take in our hand any volume; of divinity
> or school metaphysics, for instance; let us ask,
> *Does it contain any abstract reasoning concerning*
> *quantity or number?* No. *Does it contain any*

. *experimental reasoning concerning matter of fact
and existence?* No. Commit it then to the flames:
for it can contain nothing but sophistry and
illusion.

Let us now apply Hume's test with the strictest
rigour. 1. Let us take in our hand, in turn, *Winnie-the-
Pooh* and *The House at Pooh Corner*. 2. Let us, as Hume
instructs us, ask first whether they contain any
abstract reasoning concerning quantity or number,
and second whether they contain any experimental
reasoning concerning matter of fact or existence.
In both cases, the answer is a confident, indeed a
resounding, 'Yes'.

*Experimental reasoning in 'Winnie-the-Pooh'
and 'The House at Pooh Corner'*
We will take the second question first, as much of
the answer has already been supplied in the previous
pages. We need merely remind ourselves of Pooh's
scientific investigation of the nature and quantity of
the contents of the HUNNY jar, of the behaviour of
bees, and his demonstration that 'Heffalump' was a
mere name without any corresponding reality in the
outside world.

However, to put Pooh's Humean credentials beyond all possible doubt, we will remind ourselves of
three more instances of the Great Bear's experimental

---

reasoning on matters of fact and existence.

Even the most superficial Ursinian student must remember the time of the great flood which turned all our characters into temporary islanders. Having received the message – more precisely the 'missage' – that Piglet had put in a bottle, Pooh needed some kind of water transport to take him to 'one of those clever readers' who could interpret the message for him.

After some thought, he said, 'If a bottle can float, then a jar can float, and if a jar floats, I can sit on top of it, if it's a very big jar.' He acts accordingly, and soon arrives at Christopher Robin's on his craft, *The Floating Bear*.

Here we have a brief but brilliant example of the hypothetico-deductive approach to a factual problem. The first step in this approach is to form a hypothesis from which we can deduce results already obtained. Pooh does this by stating the hypothesis that a bottle *can* float. From this, we can deduce that a bottle *would* – in favourable circumstances – float. And this result has already been obtained, because the bottle has floated to Pooh. The next requirement is that the hypothesis should entail some new experimental prediction which can be either verified or refuted. Pooh predicts (1) that a jar could and would float, and (2) that he could sit on top of it if it were a very big jar. He then exposes his predictions to a test that will either verify or refute them. Once again we notice that the Great Bear frequently employs Sir Karl Popper's criterion of falsifiability; that is, he exposes a theory to an experiment which might show it to be false.

The alert and perceptive reader will notice that this instance of Pooh as experimenter also emphasizes the important fact that even a successful hypothesis may have to survive some preliminary setbacks. For Milne tells us briefly that Pooh had to try 'one or two different positions' before establishing his proper position on top of the jar.

When Pooh's hypothesis has been verified, and he has reached Christopher Robin, they then need a larger boat, to carry both of them to Piglet. Pooh swiftly solves this problem by pointing out they could use Christopher Robin's umbrella as a boat by turning it upside down.

The incautious reader may jump to the conclusion that the wobbling of the upturned umbrella – which deposited Pooh in the water – showed that Pooh's original hypothesis needed correction. But this is to forget exactly what that hypothesis was. ' "We might go in your umbrella," said Pooh.' Precisely: 'we', not 'I'. And Milne tells in the clearest terms, 'Then they both got in together, and it wobbled no longer.' Exactly what Pooh had predicted.

As we have often had occasion to be critical of Christopher Robin, we are happy to note that on this occasion he achieved a proper appreciation of Pooh. The first evidence of this appears when he contemplates *The Floating Bear*: 'the more he looked at it, the more he thought what a Brave and Clever Bear Pooh was.' He carries his appreciation from the internal to the external sphere when, seated in the no longer wobbling inverted umbrella, he announces, 'I shall call this boat *The Brain of Pooh*.'

If Christopher Robin could, for once, transcend his limitations, surely we can do at least as much.

Our third instance has a somewhat surprising source. Tigger does not ordinarily strike us as an example of scientific method, yet he provides us with a clear and elegant example. On his first appearance, he advances the hypothesis that Tiggers like everything (as food). He proceeds to test this by experimenting in turn with honey, haycorns, and thistles. Each of these disconfirms his original hypothesis. In a truly scientific spirit, Tigger keeps reformulating his hypothesis until he tries Roo's Extract of Malt, and is able to say, 'So that's what Tiggers Like!'

Mathematical reasoning in 'Pooh'

Now we turn to Hume's other question: 'Does it [any philosophical work] contain any abstract reasoning concerning quantity or number?' Here the answer is not so obvious. True, Pooh Bear tells Rabbit and Piglet, 'There's a thing called Twy-stymes,' – which we may take as a Wobbly Spelling reference to the twice-times table. But this is hardly an impressive instance of abstract reasoning concerning number. Nor are we much advanced when Milne asks Christopher Robin, 'What about nine times a hundred and seven?' And Christopher Robin's own reference to 'something called Factors' does not suggest any clear understanding of algebra.

Similarly, references to quantity are numerous but concrete, such as the amount of honey in a jar, or Pooh's dimensions compared to the dimensions of Rabbit's door.

A little reflection, however, supplies a clear affirmative answer to Hume's question. Indeed it supplies two. One is simply to remember Milne's whole strategy, which is to impart philosophical thoughts in the form of stories ostensibly written for children. (A modern parallel is Professor Daniel C. Dennett, who often presents his ideas in the form of science fiction stories.) A second answer is that Milne was illustrating John Stuart Mill's argument that mathematics were generalizations from the facts of experience.

As we shall examine Mill's mathematical theories in the next chapter, let us concentrate on the implications of the first answer. These will lead us to expect to find mathematical abstractions hidden in apparently simple and even childish anecdotes. And this, of course, is precisely what we do find. The detailed information we receive about Rabbit's friends-and-relations is a brilliant demonstration of set theory, one of the most abstruse areas of mathematics. As set theory is particularly associated with Bertrand Russell, we shall postpone detailed examination of this also to the next chapter.

I think we have done enough to establish the great opus we are investigating as acceptable in Humean terms. However, we can go further. We can show the Great Bear enunciating a totally new mathematical concept; one which, to the best of our knowledge, still remains to be explored. Consider this passage.

> 'I just like to know . . . so as I can say to myself: "I've got fourteen pots of honey left." Or fifteen, as the case may be. It's sort of comforting.'

Here we have a truly original concept, which,

once it is fully appreciated, must revolutionize all mathematical thinking. To the existing categories of number – natural, rational, irrational, real, complex, algebraic, transcendental, cardinal and ordinal – we must now add the category of comforting numbers.

It is little to the credit of philosophers and mathematicians alike that the whole area of comforting numbers remains unexplored to this day – sixty-four years after Pooh Bear's publication of it in Chapter Three of *The House at Pooh Corner*.

With this sobering thought, we pass on to the next chapter.

5

Later developments
of the Empiricist tradition

John Stuart Mill (1806–73)

John Stuart Mill is famous chiefly for his modification of the stark and simplistic Utilitarianism of his father, James Mill (1773–1836), and his father's friend, Jeremy Bentham (1748–1832). How Pooh Bear expounded this, we shall see shortly. But first we will look at his exposition of Mill's mathematical theory, which we mentioned towards the end of the last chapter.

In Chapter Nine of *Winnie-the-Pooh*, Pooh finds himself surrounded by water. Having decided that the situation is Serious and that he must have an Escape, he

> took his largest pot of honey and escaped
> with it to a broad branch of his tree, well
> above the water, and then he climbed down

again and escaped with another pot . . . and
when the whole Escape was finished, there was
Pooh sitting on his branch . . . and there, beside
him, were ten pots of honey . . .

Two days later, there was Pooh . . . and
there, beside him, were four pots of honey . . .
Three days later, there was Pooh . . . and
there, beside him, was one pot of honey.
Four days later, there was Pooh . . .

Here we have a clear example of Mill's dictum that —

All numbers must be numbers of something;
there are no such things as numbers in the
abstract.

This proposition is part of the foundation of Mill's radically empiricist theory of mathematics. Many empiricists, from Hume to Ayer, distinguished mathematical and logical truths from truths arising out of experience. Even though we may learn logical or mathematical truths from experience, there is, according to Hume and Ayer, an essential difference between them and empirical facts. This essential difference is that once we understand a mathematical or logical truth, we see that it is necessarily true without exception. Whereas empirical knowledge gives rise only to probable generalizations which might be falsified.

Mill rejected this distinction. He argued that mathematical 'truths' were empirical generalizations, like scientific 'truths'. The only difference, according to him, lay in the greater certainty of mathematical predictions.

Have we any reason to suppose Pooh Bear either accepted or rejected Mill's mathematical empiricism? Apart from the general unlikelihood that he would depart from his usual expository approach, it is particularly unlikely he would do so here. The philosophy of mathematics is notoriously an area where every known theory gives rise to problems which, if not insoluble, have not yet been solved.

We will therefore proceed to study Winnie-the-Pooh on more general aspects of Mill's philosophy. Before we do so, let us remember two important facts. Mill is generally regarded as the most eminent of Utilitarian philosophers. He is also notably a philosopher whose thought developed in depth and subtlety in the course of his life. As we should expect, the Great Bear does full justice to both these aspects of Mill.

When Pooh is taking a pot of honey as a birthday present to Eeyore, he 'absentmindedly' eats the honey on the way. Somewhat dismayed at first, he realizes that the pot itself will be 'Useful'. In his short conversation with Owl, he twice tells him the pot will be 'Useful'. And the word is used three more times to Eeyore himself, twice by Pooh and once by Piglet.

What more emphatic indication could we have that Pooh is here presenting what Mill himself called 'The creed which accepts as the foundation of morals, *Utility*, [my emphasis] or the Greatest Happiness Principle'?

Even by itself, this episode of the Useful Pot gives us a clear example of the basic premise of Utilitarian ethics. But of course it does more than that. Observant readers doubtless noticed the inverted commas round 'absentmindedly'. Those who are perceptive as well as observant will have realized why they are there.

It is manifestly absurd to suppose that the Great Bear did not know what he was doing when he ate the honey. I would argue that he ate it – to use

J. L. Austin's distinction – not only intentionally but deliberately and on purpose. By so doing, he added a demonstration of Mill's later and subtler development of Utilitarian ethics.

Two paragraphs ago, we quoted Mill on the foundation of his morality. The quotation continues –

> actions are right in proportion as they tend
> to promote happiness, wrong as they tend to
> produce the reverse of happiness. By happi-
> ness is intended pleasure, and the absence of
> pain; by unhappiness, pain, and the privation
> of pleasure.

Now we have repeated and irrefutable evidence that the food which gave Winnie-the-Pooh the greatest pleasure was honey. We have equally clear evidence that Eeyore's favourite food was thistles. It is obvious then that if Pooh had abstained from eating the honey he would have suffered that particular kind of unhappiness caused by the privation of pleasure. By eating it, he gave himself pleasure and did not deprive Eeyore of any pleasure at all. Eeyore's happiness at the end of the chapter demonstrates this beyond all reasonable doubt.

One may also of course interpret the difference of taste in relation to Mill's famous dictum, 'It is better to be a human being dissatisfied than a pig satisfied; it is better to be Socrates dissatisfied than a fool satisfied.' This sentence occurred in his discussion of the problem caused by the fact that different people choose different pleasures. Bentham had argued against any attempt to rank pleasures in any order of merit: push-pin (a children's game) was as good as poetry if it gave equal pleasure.

Mill, on the other hand, was convinced that some pleasures were of a higher quality than others. He also believed 'that those who are equally acquainted with, and equally capable of appreciating and enjoying, both, do give a most marked preference to the manner of existence which employs their higher faculties.'

Now we have already seen in Chapter Two that honey is a long-standing symbol of the highest spiritual, intellectual and social values. Thistles have an equally long history of symbolizing an unappetizing diet. Thus Pooh's marked preference for honey and Eeyore's for thistles symbolize Pooh's vast intellectual superiority, as well as his impeccable judgment in assigning the honey to himself and the Useful Pot to Eeyore.

We are aware that this comment may pain those who have a particular affection for Eeyore. To them we say that we share that affection to the full. But we do not let it blind us to the fact that Eeyore, however lovable, is simply not Pooh Bear's intellectual equal.

Before we move on, there is another aspect of Eeyore's connection with Utilitarianism which calls for a brief mention. In Chapter Six of *Winnie-the-Pooh*, Eeyore is confessing his own social limitations. He admits he lacks 'Bon-hommy ... French word meaning bonhommy'.

Those Ursinian scholars who have found time to widen their understanding of the Great Bear – and what do they know of Winnie that only Winnie know? – will remember E. C. Bentley's brief but penetrating biography:

> John Stuart Mill,
> By a mighty effort of will,
> Put aside his natural bonhommie,
> And wrote *Principles of Political Economy*.

What are we to make of this? Are we to take Eeyore as the true representative of Mill's Utilitarianism? If so, does this upgrade Eeyore or downgrade Utilitarianism? As it is our deepest desire to stimulate our readers' own philosophical explorations, and not in the slightest to choose their paths for them, we will leave this fascinating problem to them.

Let us now return to Tigger's quest for a satisfactory breakfast food. We already – on pages 420–3 and 84–5 – detailed this quest. So here it is enough to remember that he started off with a generalized desire for food, rejected several particular kinds, and ended by discovering Extract of Malt as what he really liked.

There can be no doubt that this illustrates the latest

and most sophisticated form of Mill's Utilitarianism. The great and obvious problem about Utilitarianism in its earlier and simpler form is that the concept of utility or happiness is too abstract. Most of us do not at any given moment want utility or happiness in the abstract: we want some particular thing or experience, such as a pot of honey or the experience of tasting it.

Mill provided a solution to this problem in his later version of Utilitarianism. His solution was to take into account, not only the primary idea of pleasure or happiness or utility in the abstract, but also the secondary pleasures that gave content and reality to the former. Thus Tigger's generalized desire for food, and his repeated assertion that 'Tiggers like everything', are transparent metaphors for utility etc. in the abstract, while his final settling on Extract of Malt is an equally clear metaphor for the role of secondary pleasures in giving a satisfying reality to this abstraction.

The Empiricist tradition
in the twentieth century

Bertrand Russell (1872–1970)

Just as we can regard Mill as continuing the Empiricist tradition in the nineteenth century, so we can regard Russell, the early Wittgenstein and Ayer as continuing it in the twentieth. True, they were often given more specialist labels, such as 'linguistic philosophy' for Wittgenstein and 'logical positivism' for Ayer. But Ayer himself announced in the first sentence of his Preface to the first edition of *Language, Truth and Logic*, 'The views which are put forward in this treatise derive from the doctrines of Bertrand Russell and Wittgenstein, which are themselves the logical outcome of the empiricism of Berkeley and David Hume.'

Bertrand Russell was perhaps the most wide-ranging philosopher of the twentieth century – at least so far as the English-speaking world is concerned. In addition to his strictly philosophical work, he wrote and lectured on education, sexual ethics, and the ethics of nuclear war. In his professional sphere, he made important contributions in the fields of mathematical and logical philosophy and in the theory of knowledge (epistemology). A master of clear English, he was a great popularizer of philosophy.

Like other popularizers, he was sometimes regarded with suspicion by his more austere – and less intelligible – colleagues. Nevertheless, the audience he stimulated included some who went on to become philosophers of unimpeachable academic attainment. That very eminent, and certainly not easy, philosopher, Willard van Orman Quine attested to this when he said to an audience of philosophers, 'I think many of us were drawn to our profession by Russell's books.' For its general influence, few of Russell's books were more important than his *The Problems of Philosophy*. First published in 1912, it is still a widely recommended text for university students preparing to read philosophy.

The parallels between Russell and Winnie-the-Pooh are obvious. This short exploratory work sketches the universality of the Great Bear's philosophical knowledge and understanding. Faced with such a rich, indeed bewildering, variety of choice, I have chosen just one aspect of Russell for exposition by Pooh: Set Theory, a set being a collection of objects which are members or elements of the set.

Take the following passages.

1. 'at the end, in a long line, all Rabbit's friends-and-relations.'
2. 'the smallest friend-and-relation . . . was Alexander Beetle.'
3. 'Rabbit had so many friends-and-relations, and of such different sorts and sizes, that he didn't know whether he ought to be looking for Small [a friend-and-relation who was missing] at the top of an oak-tree or in the petal of a buttercup.'
4. 'whether he [Small] was the sort of friend-and-relation who settled on one's nose, or the sort

who got trodden on by mistake.'

5. 'Small's real name was Very Small Beetle, but he was called Small for short . . . He had been staying with Christopher Robin for a few seconds, and he started round a gorse-bush for exercise, but instead of coming back the other way, as expected, he hadn't, so nobody knew where he was.'

What is all this but a graphic example of set theory? And set theory is notoriously one of the most abstract and rarefied forms of mathematics.

Let us define as Set A: all Rabbit's friends-and-relations.

Then we have:

Set Aa: consisting of one member, Alexander Beetle.

Set Ab: consisting of all Rabbit's friends-and-relations to be found at the top of an oak-tree.

Set Ac: consisting of Rabbit's friends-and-relations to be found in the petal of a buttercup.

Set Ad: consisting of Rabbit's friends-and-relations who settled on one's nose.

Set Ae: consisting of Rabbit's friends-and-relations who got trodden on by mistake.

Set Af: consisting of Rabbit's friends-and-relations who were beetles.

Set Afa: consisting of Rabbit's friends-and-relations who were large beetles.

Set Afb: consisting of Rabbit's friends-and-relations who were medium-sized beetles.

Set Afc: consisting of Rabbit's friends-and-relations who were small beetles.

Set Afc1:   consisting of Rabbit's friends-and-relations who were small beetles; whose full name was Very Small Beetle; who was usually addressed as 'Small'; who had recently been staying briefly with Christopher Robin; who had started round a gorse-bush for exercise; who had been expected to come back the other way, but had not; whose whereabouts were now unknown. NB. This set, like Aa (Alexandér Beetle), contains only one member: Very Small Beetle.

Well-informed readers will notice that Milne's formulation avoids Russell's famous paradox because he determines sets by their members – as exhaustively shown above – not by their specifying conditions. Incidentally, this also illustrates the comparatively recent distinction between 'set' and 'class'. Membership of a class is defined by sharing a concept: membership of a set may depend on an arbitrary list of qualities, as shown above in the qualities that define membership of the set whose only member is Very Small Beetle.

I think I have fulfilled the promise I made in the previous chapter to justify Pooh Bear in the most rigorously Humean terms.

Sir Alfred Ayer (1910–89)

Ayer's place here is fully justified by his own claim, quoted at the beginning of this chapter, to be following the Empiricist tradition. He is, however, more specially associated with Logical Positivism.

The hallmark of Logical Positivism was its emphasis on the Verification Principle or – more precisely – the Principle of Verifiability.

Without going into the different ways in which this principle was formulated, we may here content ourselves with saying that according to it, a statement was meaningful if and only if there was some way of testing it. The only kind of tests Logical Positivists accepted were observation, either everyday or scientific, or consistency, in the case of mathematical and logical statements.

Readers will note that this distinction between empirically observable facts and the tautological truths of mathematics and logic is in strict accord with the Empirical tradition. In practice, application of the Principle of Verifiability excluded all religious and aesthetic statements, which Logical Positivists labelled 'metaphysical' and dismissed as neither true nor false but simply meaningless.

For Winnie-the-Pooh's demonstration of the Principle of Verifiability we turn again to the episode of the HUNNY jar. Pooh does not explicitly enunciate the proposition, 'There is a jar of honey on my larder shelf', but it is clearly implied. We need not again describe the thorough, and peculiarly appropriate verification process he follows before he is satisfied that the proposition is both meaningful and true. Indeed we may say that he also illustrates an early and often quoted definition of the principle: Moritz Schlick's 'the meaning of a proposition consists in its method of verification.' Pooh Bear would surely have agreed that the proposition 'There is a jar of honey' could – and should – be verified by his having the experience of eating the honey.

The Verification Principle in anything like its original form has been abandoned, partly because there were problems about reconciling it with itself – was the Verification Principle itself empirical or tautological? – partly because no one succeeded in formulating it in a way that did not include too much or too little. Similar problems arose in connection with the Principle of Falsifiability, to which we now turn.

Sir Karl Raimund Popper (1902–94)

Sir Karl Popper has made important contributions in several branches of philosophy, but here we shall concentrate on his Principle of Falsifiability. Unlike the Principle of Verifiability, this was not intended to distinguish between meaningful and meaningless propositions, but between those that are scientific and those that are non-scientific ('metaphysical' in Popper's special use of the word).

Popper was considering how to demarcate science from non-science. Many scientific statements are generalizations of the sort usually called 'laws of science'. Now no empirical generalization can ever be absolutely certain, though of course it may attain such a high degree of probability that we are justified in relying on it. When we go to bed at night, we are confident that the sun will rise the next day. It always has, not only in our own experience, but in the earliest human records, and, if astronomical calculations are correct, for billions of years before human records or even humanity existed.

Nevertheless, this, like all arguments from experience (inductive arguments), *might* prove false. Some unpredicted catastrophe might prevent the sun from rising. Similarly, however many instances we may find to support a law of science, there is always the possibility, however remote, that some contradictory fact may be discovered. Given the fact that no general proposition of fact can be certain, as opposed to highly probable, how are we to distinguish scientific statements from those that are not scientific?

Popper's answer was that while no accumulation of instances could prove a theory correct, one counter-instance could disprove it, at least in part. To take a famous example, however many white swans ornithologists counted, without encountering an exception, they could not prove the proposition 'All swans are white.' But *one* well-supported example of a black swan would prove the proposition false.

In Popper's view, any statement that claims to be scientific must in principle be capable of being falsified if it is indeed incorrect. For example, when an astronomer predicts the appearance of a comet on a particular date in a particular part of the sky, that statement is open to falsification, if the astronomer has got things wrong. This, therefore, is a scientific statement by Popper's criteria. If, on the other hand, someone says that all our actions are really controlled by little green Martians, but that these are and always will be totally undetectable, then that is not a scientific statement, because no conceivable test could falsify it.

Our readers must already be well aware that the attitude of Winnie-the-Pooh is deeply scientific; so indeed is the attitude of most of his companions. But for an example of Popperian falsifiability nothing is more appropriate than – yet again – Tigger's approach to breakfast. This we will now re-examine.

Asked (by Pooh Bear) whether Tiggers like honey, Tigger replies, 'They like everything.' Now, following Popper, we may note that this proposition could not be verified beyond all doubt. Even though the context clearly restricts 'everything' to every kind of food, however many instances Tigger sampled and liked, there would always be the possibility that some food remained untried, perhaps even uninvented. On the other hand, just one instance of a food he did not like would falsify his proposition.

In a truly scientific spirit, Tigger submits his proposition to the risk of falsification. And indeed his first experiment does falsify it. Lest any reader should fail to grasp the Popperian relevance of this episode, we are shown Tigger replicating the experiment with haycorns and thistles. Pooh Bear himself sums up the results in a memorable Hum:

He doesn't like honey and haycorns and thistles
Because of the taste and because of the bristles.
And all the good things which an animal likes
Have the wrong sort of swallow or too many spikes.

The final result appears that, far from liking everything, Tigger finds only Extract of Malt acceptable.
But the important fact is that he has reached this
conclusion by a truly scientific process.

Ludwig Wittgenstein (1889–1951)

'Well,' said Owl, 'the customary procedure
in such cases is as follows.'
   'What does Crustimoney Proseedcake mean?'
said Pooh. 'For I am a Bear of Very Little Brain,
and long words Bother me.'

Incredible as it must now seem to any reader who
has reached this point, many Ursinian students have
taken Pooh's statement at its face value, and have
even referred to it as evidence of his linguistic limitations. It is, of course, a highly effective dramatization
of paragraph 4.026 of Wittgenstein's *Tractatus Logico-
Philosophicus*, which begins, 'The meaning of simple
signs (words) must be explained to us if we are to
understand them.'
   Any possible doubt that Pooh is alluding to this

passage is dispelled when we read on. Owl proceeds:

> 'It means the Thing to Do.'
>   'As long as it means that, I don't mind,'
> said Pooh humbly.

Here we see Owl converting his somewhat obscure first utterance into a clear proposition. Thus he demonstrates (1) the need to explain words, and also (2) illustrates the second sentence in Wittgenstein's paragraph 4.026, which goes, 'With propositions, however, we make ourselves understood.' Exactly what Owl has done.

Many Pooh students have felt that study of any other philosophers is a waste of time, and may therefore need the information that Wittgenstein divided the *Tractatus* into numbered and subnumbered paragraphs, often as short as one sentence. I must admit that a dismissive attitude to other philosophers can find support in Wittgenstein himself; for he wrote, 'Most of the propositions and questions to be found in philosophical works are not false but nonsensical. Consequently we cannot give any answer to questions of this kind, but can only point out that they are nonsensical. Most of the propositions and questions of philosophers arise from our failure to understand the logic of our language' (4.003). Nevertheless, I would remind readers tempted to act on this principle that by doing so they will cut themselves off from even approaching a full appreciation of the Great Bear himself.

For example, unless we had read Wittgenstein's comment about philosophers' nonsensical questions, we could hardly see the clear reference to it in Pooh's 'Cottleston Pie', which, as all Pooh readers know, ends

> Cottleston, Cottleston, Cottleston Pie,
> Why does a chicken, I don't know why.
> Ask me a riddle and I reply:
> *'Cottleston, Cottleston, Cottleston Pie.'*

'Why does a chicken' is a strikingly obvious example of the sort of question Wittgenstein condemns as nonsensical and consequently unanswerable. Pooh's superficially irrelevant answer recognizes it as such, and smilingly dismisses it.

Though Pooh dismisses the nonsensical question, we must not fall into the error of lightly dismissing this passage. Three elements need to be analysed:

1. The question itself.
2. The punctuation of the question.
3. The content of Pooh's reply, and its implications.

1. The question begins in a way that leads us to expect it will be completed with the traditional

words, so as to form the old riddle, 'Why does a chicken cross the road?' Inviting the reply, 'Because it wants to get to the other side.' So powerfully is this expectation created, that many readers seem unaware that it is not fulfilled. Others, more alert but equally misguided, interpret the truncated question as a mere abbreviation, requiring us to complete it with the traditional words. A moment's reflection will convince us that this cannot be the answer.

The question in its traditional form is perfectly rational, and the traditional reply answers it rationally. Therefore it cannot possibly be an example of a nonsensical question. Nor is it a philosophical question. But the question *as actually presented in the song* – 'Why does a chicken' – is both nonsensical and the sort of question that appears all too often in philosophical works. Thus it illustrates Wittgenstein's point perfectly.

2. Many readers have commented on the punctuation of this line. Milne's great *opus* is meticulously punctuated throughout; yet here we find a comma instead of the obviously necessary question mark. Why? Because the author was warning us that this simply is not a genuine question. The typographical device indicates it is a nonsensical or pseudo-question.

3. Pooh's response, 'Cottleston Pie', performs two

functions. We have already seen that it recognizes the nonsensical nature of the question. It does more though. The repeated reference to pie brings us down to earth, and back to the necessities and delights of the real world after the vacuous bombinations of a certain kind of philosopher.

We have previously noted that Pooh is essentially an active thinker, so we need not point to any one instance that illustrates Wittgenstein's dictum, 'Philosophy is not a body of doctrine but an activity' (4.112). That 'All philosophy is a critique of language' is also repeatedly illustrated in the Milnean opus, but here we need some more detailed analysis.

Take these passages. *Winnie-the-Pooh*, Chapter One:

> 'He's Winnie-ther-Pooh. Don't you know what *"ther"* means?'
> 'Ah, yes, now I do,' I said quickly; and I hope you do too, because it is all the explanation you are going to get.

Chapter Six, where Eeyore explains 'Here we go round the mulberry bush' as 'Bon-hommy'; and most striking of all, Rabbit's statement, with reference to the proposed kidnapping of Roo, that

> 'We say "*Aha!*" so that Kanga knows that *we* know where Baby Roo is. "*Aha!*" means "We'll

tell you where Baby Roo is, if you promise to go
away from the Forest and never come back." '

These three passages – and there are many others
– clearly refer to Wittgenstein's 'In philosophy the
question, "What do we actually use this word or
this proposition for?" repeatedly leads to valuable
insights' (6.211).

A rapid survey reveals some of these insights.
The first passage shows that even in so clear a work
as *Winnie-the-Pooh* a key concept may be unexplained.
Why? Wittgenstein himself offers two possible explanations. In the very second paragraph of the Preface to
the *Tractatus* he tells us, 'The whole sense of the book
might be summed up in the following words: what can
be said at all can be said clearly, and what we cannot
talk about we must pass over in silence.'

But while we should certainly, and with more
reason, imitate the humility of Pooh Bear, we should
not abandon the search for meaning too easily. Let
us remember that in a later work, *Philosophical Investigations*, Wittgenstein wrote, also in the Preface, 'I
should not like my writing to spare other people
the trouble of thinking. But, if possible, to stimulate
someone to thoughts of his own.'

Both Eeyore's daring equation of 'Here we go
round the mulberry bush' with 'Bon-hommy' and
Rabbit's even more audacious loading '*Aha!*' with
such a complex message to Kanga illustrate Wittgen-

stein's point about usage. As usual, they carry more than one message, more even than one Wittgensteinian message.

We all remember that after Rabbit had explained his use of 'Aha!'

> Pooh went into a corner and tried saying 'Aha!'
> in that sort of voice. Sometimes it seemed to
> him that it did mean what Rabbit said, and
> sometimes it seemed to him that it didn't.
> 'I suppose it's just practice,' he thought. 'I
> wonder if Kanga will have to practise too so
> as to understand it.'

Here Pooh is putting to us precisely the same thoughts that Wittgenstein expressed in paragraph 4.002: 'Everyday language is a part of the human organism and is no less complicated than it.' And later in the same paragraph, 'The tacit conventions on which the understanding of everyday language depends are enormously complicated.' Pooh brings out the second idea with particular force when he asks whether Kanga will need practice to understand, for without the appropriate practice, whether by formal training or real world experience, we cannot understand any messages.

Moreover, one of the tacit conventions is that there should be suitable connections between utterances and the situations in which they are made. Pooh has pointed to the emptiness of an utterance

– in this case, Rabbit's heavily laden 'Aha' – when made without the proper accompanying situation. 'We could [said Pooh] say "Aha!" even if we hadn't stolen Baby Roo.'

Far from understanding the vital point Pooh is making, the self-important but intellectually obtuse Rabbit seems to think Pooh is actually recommending this absurd course of action, and –

> 'Pooh,' said Rabbit kindly, 'you haven't any brain.'
> 'I know,' said Pooh humbly.

A part of his humility must have arisen from realizing that enlightening Rabbit was a task beyond even his powers. In his post-Pooh *Philosophical Investigations*, Wittgenstein commented: 'An unsuitable type of expression is a sure way of remaining in a state of confusion' (section 339).

Though the Pooh stories are full of examples that demonstrate the philosophical importance of language, the richest sources are those episodes that involve Wol, or Owl, as he is known to mere mortals.

We have already looked at the very first of these, and examined two aspects of it: the need for words to be explained, and the use of propositions in making ourselves understood. But there is, of course, more to it.

Pooh himself prepares us to meet a being of outstanding knowledge:

'And if anyone knows anything about anything,' said Bear to himself, 'it's Owl who
knows something about something,' he said,
'or my name's not Winnie-the-Pooh,' he said.
'Which it is,' he added. 'So there you are.'

Pooh's strongly worded tribute is something we should constantly bear in mind when we are considering Wol. Remembering it, we should be safe against any temptation to take Wol less than seriously as a great mind.

A proper attitude to Wol is, or should be, confirmed, even before we meet him, by the notices outside his door. Every true Ursinian knows these two notices by heart.

Underneath the knocker there was a notice which said:

PLES RING IF AN RNSER IS REQIRD.

Underneath the bell-pull there was a notice which said:

PLEZ CNOKE IF AN RNSR IS NOT REQID.

Leaving aside for the moment the matter of Wobbly Spelling, we observe that these notices fulfil all the relevant Wittgensteinian criteria. They say what they

have to say clearly, and this is partly because, syntactically and semantically, they follow the normally accepted tacit conventions of everyday language: if we find a notice outside a front door, we expect it to give us information about the person or persons dwelling in the house, especially perhaps about how to contact them. This is precisely what Wol's notices do. They do it clearly, and they cover all reasonably foreseeable contingencies.

Once contact is made, and Pooh has put the problem to Wol, Wol answers,

> 'Well, the customary procedure in such cases
> is as follows.'

Before reconsidering Pooh's request for explanation, we must analyse Wol's utterance. His reference to 'customary procedure' clearly implies that he is familiar with the ways of dealing with such problems. This is confirmed by the promptness of his

reply. This in turn confirms Pooh's high opinion of him.

Now let us look again at Pooh's insistence on an explanation. Does this imply that Wol's original statement was culpably obscure? Certainly not. If it did, it would blur the whole Wittgensteinian point that Pooh is making. It was precisely *simple* signs (my emphasis) that Wittgenstein said must be explained. Pooh's reference to long words is merely part of Socratic role-playing.

It is not, however, only this. Wol repeatedly appears a master of language. Yet he seldom solves real world problems. How can we explain this discrepancy? Though *Winnie-the-Pooh* was published in 1926, and *The House at Pooh Corner* in 1928, we had to wait until the posthumous publication of Wittgenstein's *Philosophical Investigations* in 1953 for an answer. Section 109 ends with the words, 'Philosophy is a battle against the bewitchment of our intelligence by means of language.'

In so far as Wol had a role relevant to Wittgenstein – and this is only part of his significance – it was to exemplify that bewitchment. This is not at all to downgrade him. Only a truly massive mind combined with powerful eloquence could embody the full force of linguistic enchantment. Only the even more powerful philosophic intellect of the Great Bear could win the battle against that bewitchment.

We should note too that, on one important occasion, Wol shows his awareness of the situation. I refer, of course, to the occasion when a storm trapped Pooh, Piglet and Wol in Wol's own house. The problem was how to get out. What does Wol do? He says,

> 'That is the Problem, Piglet, to which I am
> asking Pooh to give his mind.'

And when Pooh produces a brilliant and eminently practicable solution, Wol comments,

> 'Astute and Helpful Bear.'

This passage not only emphatically asserts Pooh's pre-eminence, but also highlights Wol's magnanimity in acknowledging it. It does honour to both these great minds. And also to Wittgenstein for so ably elucidating the situation.

Having stayed for a long time with the inheritors of the Empirical traditions, we now pass on to the wilder and cloudier regions of German philosophy.

6

Pooh and the German philosophers: Kant, Hegel, Nietzsche

Immanuel Kant (1724–1804)

Exploring yet again that extraordinarily rich episode of Pooh Bear and the bees, let us reconsider, now from a Kantian point of view, two utterances of Pooh: 'The only reason for being a bee that I know of is making honey . . . And the only reason for making honey is so as *I* can eat it.'

Incredible though it is, we must admit that some Ursinian students have read this as evidence of limited intelligence and even gluttony. It is, of course, – naturally among other things – an obvious teaching device for explaining Kant's basic principle that our knowledge is strictly conditioned by the constraints of our own minds. Pooh's (assumed) inability to con-

ceive of bees as anything but honey producers, and
honey except as food for him, represents Kant's doctrine of our inability to conceive of the world except
in terms of space, time and causality.

Pooh goes on to illustrate Kant's key distinction
between things as we know them ('phenomena') and
things in themselves ('noumena').

' "You never can tell with bees," said Winnie-
the-Pooh.' We have previously looked at this dictum
from a Cartesian point of view. But it is also a clear
reference to Kant's basic teaching that things in
themselves (noumena) are unknowable.

Thus in three brief and brilliant sentences the
Great Bear has clarified two basic concepts of Kant's
philosophy.

Moreover, Pooh's use of a familiar object like
bees to make this point is itself highly Kantian.
For Kant admitted that minds not naturally attuned
to abstract thought would need concrete examples,
just as, in his own phrase, an infant needs a go-cart.
Pooh, who is addressing a general audience, always
provides such go-carts.

Kant also prophetically acknowledged Pooh as
one of his heirs when he wrote, 'To these deserving
men, who so happily combine profundity of view
with lucidity of exposition – a talent which I myself
am not conscious of possessing – I leave the task
of removing any obscurity which may still adhere
to the statement of my doctrines.' What more obvi-

ous, and generous, description of Pooh could there be?

Notice also in the phrase 'these deserving men' the clear echo of Wol's 'Astute and Helpful Bear'.

From time to time we have commented critically on the blindness of Ursinian scholars. In fairness to them, we must call attention to the equal and equally culpable blindness of Kantian scholars. We have searched their tomes in vain for any reference to this striking prophecy by the philosopher they claim as their special field of expertise.

Another interesting and somewhat controversial reference to Kant's theory of phenomena occurs in Chapter Three of *Winnie-the-Pooh*, 'In Which Pooh and Piglet go Hunting and Nearly Catch a Woozle'. Piglet asks whether the tracks they are following are Woozle tracks. Pooh answers, '. . . You can never tell with paw-marks.'

Ursinian scholars are sharply divided in their interpretation of this statement. The obvious problem is that paw-marks seem clearly phenomenal, objects we perceive in space and time. Yet Pooh expresses a scepticism that seems to belong to the (Kantianly) unknowable world of things in themselves (noumena).

Some scholars, mainly Kantians, explain this by stressing the word 'with' in Pooh's sentence. Rightly reminding us that Pooh always chooses his words with the greatest care, they argue that he is not denying that you can *'tell'* paw-marks, that is, recognize them as phenomenal objects. The insertion of 'with' indicates that we cannot make the impossible leap from the visible phenomenal paw-marks to the unknowable noumenon lying behind them: in this case the Woozle. They further support this argument by pointing out that the Woozle is never found or even described. This, they say, is compelling evidence that it stands for the world of noumena.

Other scholars, mainly non-Kantians, take a more radical view, and argue that Pooh is expressing scepticism of even phenomenal knowledge.

As the last thing we want is to do our readers' thinking for them, we leave them to decide which interpretation they find more convincing.

The great Jar of HUNNY episode is also capable of a Kantian interpretation. Pooh's thorough examination of the contents revealed that they were indeed honey all the way. Alerted now to a Kantian view, our readers will have no difficulty in interpreting this to mean that however thoroughly we explore our world, our perceptions can never transcend the limits of phenomena.

Those readers who also remember the symbolical values of honey (wisdom, truth, goodness) will recognize, with admiration but hardly surprise, that Pooh Bear is transcending the limits of phenomena even in the act of illustrating them, and is thus transcending the transcendental philosopher, Kant.

Pooh Bear's critique of Kantian ethics

Tigger's search for a food that he really likes and Pooh Bear's eating the honey before giving the Useful – but now empty – Pot to Eeyore are a vivid critique of the main problem of Kantian ethics. The best-known version of Kant's basic moral principle, the Categorical Imperative, runs as follows: 'Act only on that maxim which you can at the same time will to become a universal law.' At once we face the problem: how can we fulfil Kant's criterion while choosing a suitable food or gift for a particular person? Anyone who made it a maxim to give everyone honey, would have dissatisfied the recipient (Eeyore) in the given example. But if we make a separate choice for each recipient, we are not willing each choice to become a universal law.

It may be answered that this is a quite unreal problem, and that the obvious solution is to act on the maxim that we should give the sort of gifts the recipients will enjoy. Or – as that formula would allow us to give a case of whisky to an alcoholic or a gun to a psychopath – we could say we should give gifts which were appropriate to the recipient. But that merely means we ought to give what we ought to give. True but not very helpful. In other words, Winnie-the-Pooh has exposed what Alasdair MacIntyre called 'the logical emptiness of the test of the categorical imperative' (*A Short History of Ethics*, p.198).

Obviously Kant needed Winnie-the-Pooh to clarify his own obscure prose. And we have just seen the Great Bear expose the unreality of Kant's ethical foundation. Nevertheless, we must acknowledge that Kant dominated German, indeed European, philosophy for at least a century, and is still a powerful influence today.

By far the most influential of his German successors was Hegel, to whom we now turn.

Georg Wilhelm Friedrich Hegel (1770–1831)

Before beginning to analyse Hegel's philosophy, I feel I should give my readers two warnings. 1. Bertrand Russell commented that Hegel 'is . . . the hardest to understand of all the great philosophers.' Hegel himself said, 'I shall try to teach philosophy to speak German.' It was not very clear German. His reputation is well conveyed by the possibly apocryphal story that on his deathbed Hegel himself said, 'Only one man understood me – and he didn't really understand me.' 2. Difficulties of subject matter are compounded by different translations of key terms in his philosophy. His *Geist* is sometimes translated 'Mind'; sometimes 'Spirit'. I decided that the true flavour of Hegel was best conveyed by retaining these differences rather than by producing a superficial consistency.

Readers then should not despair if they find parts of this section less perspicuous than the rest of the book. Still less, of course, should they accuse either Milne or Pooh of falling below their usual standards of pellucid exposition.

We may begin our investigation of Milne-Pooh's exposition of Hegel by considering the first and last paragraphs of *Winnie-the-Pooh*, Chapter One, and the last paragraph of the same work's last chapter. In order, these read as follows:

1. 'Here is Edward Bear, coming downstairs now, bump, bump, bump, on the back of his head, behind Christopher Robin. It is, as far as he knows, the only way of coming downstairs, but sometimes he feels that there really is another way, if only he could stop bumping for a moment and think of it. And then he feels that perhaps there isn't. Anyhow, here he is at the bottom, and ready to be introduced to you. Winnie-the-Pooh.'
2. '. . . I heard Winnie-the-Pooh – *bump, bump, bump* – going up the stairs behind him.'
3. '. . . I heard Winnie-the-Pooh – *bump, bump, bump* – going up the stairs behind him.'

Viewing these passages through Hegelian spectacles, what do we see? At first, we may notice only the identity of the second and third and the contrast of both with the first. This may remind us – rather vaguely – of Hegel's concept of that identity-in-difference which it is the task of philosophy to discover. But this is hardly satisfactory. Let us think again, and this time let us think particularly of Hegel's Philosophy of Mind.

Pooh and Hegel's Philosophy of Mind

At once, all becomes clear. We see the obvious – though hitherto unnoticed – fact that these three paragraphs sum up Hegel's three stages in the development of Mind (or Spirit): Mind Subjective, Mind Objective, and Mind Absolute. The following analysis should clarify the position for those not immediately convinced.

Right at the beginning, we notice that the Great Bear is first referred to as 'Edward Bear'. Only at the end of this fairly long paragraph is he 'introduced' – and we must pay full attention to that significantly chosen word – as 'Winnie-the-Pooh'. This indeterminateness about the correct name obviously exemplifies Hegel's dictum that in its rudimentary stage Mind is 'the idea in its indeterminateness'.

The idea of the Subjective Mind's indeterminateness is further developed in the Bear's vague notions about other possible ways of coming downstairs. (I hope it is no longer necessary to remind readers that this ignorance is simply assumed as a peda-

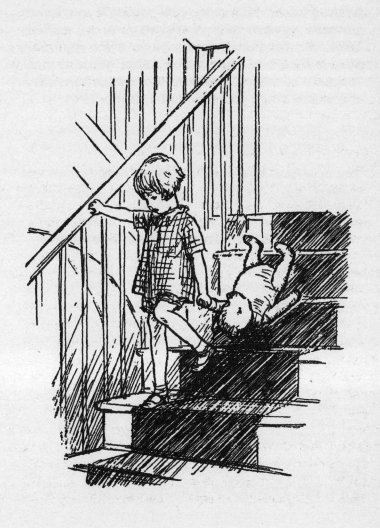

gogic device.) Moreover, this apparent confusion contains the first and second steps of a Hegelian triad, the three-stage model he so often uses. The triad consisted of a thesis (first statement); antithesis (opposite of thesis); and synthesis (which reconciled the contradiction on some higher level). Thus

1. There are other ways of coming downstairs.
2. There are not other ways of coming downstairs.

The expected third stage is delayed until later in the chapter, when we find Pooh himself demonstrating that

3. There is another way of coming down a tree.

To those who object that another way of descending trees is not a satisfactory synthesis of the two preceding propositions of the triad, supporters of this interpretation point to the last line of the Complaining Song Pooh sang as he climbed the tree in pursuit of honey.

It's a very funny thought that, if Bears were Bees,
They'd build their nests at the *bottom* of trees.
And that being so (if the Bees were Bears),
We shouldn't have to climb up all these stairs.

Here, they say, is incontrovertible proof that the Great Bear himself was equating trees with stairs.

Another school of thought finds the resolution in our second quotation, at the end of Chapter One. Here the method is the same but the direction is opposite: up instead of down. On this interpretation, the resolution is

3. There is another way of going upstairs.

As Hegel is the most eminent example of dialectical idealism, it is unsurprising to find many interpretations that are themselves in dialectical opposition. We are happy to leave to our readers the Hegelian exercise of reconciling them in a higher unity.

There is, however, another interpretation of this passage which by no means excludes the one just mentioned, but rather transcends it. Before coming to this interpretation, we must remember that we are dealing with a work as distinguished for rhetorical skill as for philosophical profundity. One aspect of the rhetorical skill lies in the precise placing of particular passages. The first and last paragraphs of a chapter always carry a special weight of significance. In the case of the last paragraph, that significance is usually related to what the chapter contains. Now Chapter One contains the episode of Pooh Bear and the bees, an episode whose multifaceted richness we have amply demonstrated. What follows?

In the context of Hegelian philosophy, the answer

evidently is that the paragraph in question illustrates
the development from the first to the second stage of
Mind. We have now reached Mind Objective. Hegel
tells us that this stage is

> In the form of *reality*; realized, i.e. in a *world*
> produced and to be produced by it: in this
> world freedom presents itself under the shape
> of necessity.

How vividly and powerfully Pooh has demonstrated
Hegel's concept in the bee episode. It is Pooh's
mind that notices the buzzing, interprets it, acts on
his interpretation and so produces the world of this
episode. This precisely fulfils Hegel's first criterion.

The second criterion – that freedom will show
itself here as necessity – is fulfilled with equal precision. Pooh demonstrates freedom by climbing the
tree and flying with his balloon. Necessity appears
starkly in his falls from both.

Now we come to our third passage. We hope
none of our readers will halt at the trivial truth that
it is verbally identical with the second. Here again,
placing and context are all-important. By the time the
Ursinian students have reached the end of *Winnie-the-
Pooh*, aided we hope by our simple commentary, they
must be awesomely aware of the Great Brain of the
Great Bear. They will then find it easy to recognize
that this second ascent of the stairs represents the

third and final stage in the development of Mind.
We have reached Mind Absolute.

Hegel describes it thus:

> . . . that unity of mind as objectivity and of
> mind as ideality and concept, which essentially
> and actually is and forever produces itself,
> mind in its absolute truth. This is *Mind Absolute*.

The evidence for this lies not so much in any single
passage or episode as in that massive and complex
totality that we call the World of Pooh. And this itself
is typically Hegelian. To him, the whole was infinitely
more than the sum of its parts. Indeed, the parts
were intelligible only in so far as they belonged to
the whole. As he himself put it, 'The true is the
whole.'

Nor are these the only passages that show the
development of the three stages of Mind. Christopher
Robin's 'Pooh couldn't [catch the Heffalump] because he hasn't any brain,' is an obvious hyperbole
for the confused first state of mind – one, alas, in
which Christopher Robin is permanently stuck.

Given this clue, no one should have any difficulty in interpreting the description of Pooh as 'a
Bear of Very Little Brain' as a similarly exaggerated
reference to the second stage in the development
of Mind. Our argument is confirmed beyond all
reasonable doubt by Pooh's own confirmation that

he is 'a Bear of Enormous Brain': an incontestable illustration of Mind Absolute.

If there are still those who remain unconvinced, we must sadly attribute this to their remaining stuck in the muddle-headedness – indeterminateness in Hegel's terminology – of Mind Subjective.

The truly alert and well-informed reader will have noticed that Pooh's recognition of himself as a Bear of Enormous Brain has another Hegelian function. Professor F. C. Coplestone sums up a major element of Hegel by saying, 'Philosophical reason comes to see the whole history of the cosmos and the whole history of man [*sic*] as the self-unfolding of the Absolute. And this knowledge is the Absolute's knowledge of itself.' Can any rational being doubt that this self-knowledge of the Absolute is instanced by Pooh's knowledge of himself as a Great Brain?

We may support this further by remarking that Pooh's own self-denigrating descriptions of himself as, for example, 'a Bear of No Brain at All', may be construed, not only in the most obvious way as a Socratic strategy: in a Hegelian context, we must remember that 'Spirit . . . in its second phase separates itself from itself and makes this second aspect its own polar opposite.' That is, the Enormous Brain makes itself its polar opposite: No Brain at All.

We now turn to a philosopher of a totally different kind, but one who will also test Pooh's expository powers to the utmost.

Friedrich Nietzsche (1844–1900)

> Isn't it funny
> How a bear likes honey?
> Buzz! Buzz! Buzz!
> I wonder why he does?

We have already seen several answers to the second question posed in this riddling rhyme, but other answers remain for us to explore. The most obvious Nietzschean reference is the sentence in *Twilight of the Idols* where Ralph Waldo Emerson is specially praised as 'a man [who] instinctively feeds on pure ambrosia and leaves alone the indigestible in things.' Who can doubt that Emerson's ambrosia is equivalent to Pooh's honey?

Similarly, Pooh's teleological approach when he insists that making honey is the only reason for being a bee parallels Nietzsche's 'the tree existed only for these fruits'. This parallel is even more striking when we remember precisely what fruits Nietzsche was talking about. The fruits he meant were individuals, and where shall we find a more striking group of genuine individuals than in the World of Pooh?

Moreover in his balloon flight, Pooh clearly demonstrated Nietzsche's criterion of freedom. 'How is freedom measured, in individuals as in nations? By the resistance which has to be overcome, by the efforts it costs to stay *aloft*.'

Nietzsche was an exceptionally personal philosopher, so it is interesting to find the life-style he recommends has so many similarities with the Great Bear's. Once Pooh has been introduced as 'Winnie-the-Pooh', he appears full grown. There is no suggestion he was ever a bear-cub. No hint of parents. What is this but an illustration of Nietzsche's claim that 'everything of the first rank must be *causa sui*' (its own cause)?

Again, at the beginning of the Pooh story, we learn that, 'Winnie-the-Pooh lived in a forest all by himself . . .' This clearly bears out Nietzsche's maxim: 'To live alone one must be an animal or a god – says Aristotle. There is yet a third case: one must be both – a *philosopher.*'

A well-informed but somewhat obtuse reader might now enquire whether Pooh diminishes his philosophical stature when he invites Piglet to share his dwelling. For three separate reasons, the answer is certainly not. First, this invitation is given and accepted at the end of the penultimate chapter. By that time, the Great Bear's intellectual pre-eminence has been thoroughly established. In Nietzschean terms, he is clearly a Superbear. Secondly, he is also in Aristotelian terms a Magnanimous Bear, to whom this generous act of friendship comes naturally. Thirdly, however much Nietzsche praised solitude, there is a long and honoured tradition of great philosophers taking a favourite pupil to reside with them. And Piglet, despite his intellectual short-

comings, was Pooh's choice for this high honour.

We doubt, however, whether even daily communion with Pooh will make Piglet more than a faithful but often uncomprehending disciple. The episode we are now about to consider strongly supports this picture of the Pooh-Piglet relationship.

Returning to Pooh's exposition of Nietzsche, we naturally think of that passage at the beginning of *The House at Pooh Corner* where, on a snowy day, Pooh, having discovered Piglet is out, says, 'I shall have to go a fast Thinking Walk by myself. Bother!' A vividly concrete realization of Nietzsche's brilliant phrase defining the contemplative life as 'taking a walk with ideas and friends'. Pooh's Thinking Walk is clearly a walk with ideas, while his 'Bother!' shows his regret that on this occasion his Thinking Walk will not also be a walk with a friend. Fortunately there were other occasions when ideas and friends were both present.

Later in the same chapter, for example, Pooh is practising a Good Hum, such as is Hummed Hopefully to Others; in this instance, to Piglet. Those unfamiliar with Nietzsche may wonder what a Hum, even a Good Hum, has to do with philosophy; but those who know *The Gay Science* will remember that it has a Prelude of sixty-three 'German Rhymes' and an Appendix of fourteen 'Songs of Prince Vogelfrei'. So nothing could be more Nietzschean than a philosophical hum.

While Pooh is practising this Good Hum, Piglet,

who is not enjoying the snow, suggests the practice could be carried out at home. Pooh replies, '. . . it's a special Outdoor Song which Has To Be Sung In The Snow.'

Three points are worth noting in this episode. First, with regard to Piglet, we see that his attitude displays just that combination of loyalty with incomprehension which is so characteristic of him. Secondly, Pooh Bear's obviously joyous proclamation –

> And nobody
> KNOWS-tiddely-pom,
> How cold my
> TOES-tiddely-pom
> How cold my
> TOES-tiddeley-pom
> Are
> Growing –

exemplifies Nietzsche's 'Yes-saying without reservation, even to suffering'. Finally, we may round off this section of Pooh's exposition of Nietzsche by remarking that here he gives us a particularly striking example of Nietzsche's dictum, 'Only ideas *won by walking* have any value.'

As with so many of the philosophers we have considered, if we were to pursue and analyse all the Nietzschean references, explicit and implicit, in the *Pooh* books, we should have to expand one section of one chapter to a whole volume. Let us briefly draw

our readers' attention to a few of these references,
and then finish this section with a more detailed
examination of *Thus Spake Zarathustra*, which offers
perhaps the richest material to the Ursinian scholar.

We may therefore mention in passing that
the happy stateless culture of Pooh's society
exemplifies Nietzsche's dictum: 'Culture and the
state are antagonists.' Pooh himself is obviously just
the sort of companion Nietzsche yearned for: 'with
whom I might be cheerful!'

Nietzsche and Rabbit
When Pooh Bear has promised to find Eeyore's missing tail, he consults Owl. 'If anyone knows anything about anything, it's Owl who knows something about something.' Rabbit also turns to Owl as the natural interpreter of the mysterious message –

GON OUT
BACKSON
BISY
BACKSON

C.R.

Rabbit justifies his appeal by saying, 'Owl, you and I have brains. The others have fluff. If there is any thinking to be done in this Forest – and when I say thinking I mean *thinking* – you and I must do it.' Owl agrees. Nothing could be more obvious than the reference to Nietzsche's 'Rationality was at that time divined as a *saviour*.' Any possible doubt is removed when we remember he was talking about Socrates: the practical failure of Owl's elegantly rational approach dramatizes Nietzsche's often – as in this context – critical attitude to Socratic rationalism.

At the beginning of this modest little prolegomenon to the philosophical branch of Ursinian studies, we pointed out that, though the Great Bear is the principal exemplar and expositor of philosophy in Milne's masterpiece, he is not the only one. Let us look at the following passage, from the beginning of Chapter Five of *The House at Pooh Corner*.

> It was going to be one of Rabbit's busy days.
> As soon as he woke up he felt important, as if
> everything depended upon him. It was just the
> day for Organizing Something, or for Writing a
> Notice Signed Rabbit . . . It was a Captainish
> sort of day, when everybody said, 'Yes, Rabbit'
> and 'No, Rabbit,' and waited until he had told
> them.

This passage reveals Rabbit as an example of the bureaucratic mind; even as a potential dictator. A benevolent dictator, no doubt, but certainly a dangerous enemy to the free, co-operative harmony of the World of Pooh. Fortunately, his plans always fail. And they fail because, as Nietzsche said, 'power *makes stupid*'.

Zarathustra and honey
If there is one thing that even the most superficial reader of Winnie-the-Pooh knows it is Pooh's passion for honey. It would be merely tedious to repeat

instances. By now, I hope that all readers are aware
of the multifarious philosophical meanings borne by
this great image. They will naturally expect to find
more references in Nietzsche than the brief parallel
with Emerson's ambrosia mentioned above. They will
not be disappointed. 'All joy wants . . . honey,' wrote
Nietzsche, and he continually repeats this message.

Of course, readers familiar with *Thus Spake Zarathustra* will have been waiting impatiently for our
author's explication of the most obvious of all relevant passages, the chapter entitled 'The Honey
Offering'. At its very beginning, we read that though
Zarathustra is without human companions there are
friendly animals with whom he talks. He even tells
them, 'Your advice is admirable.' What is more
impressive, he acts on it.

While it is perfectly clear that this chapter is full
of Ursinian references, we must admit that problems
confront us when we try to work them out in detail.
For example, the chapter opens with Zarathustra in
friendly and apparently equal conversation with 'his
animals'. Yet when he has taken their advice and
climbed to the summit of the mountain, he sends
them home. When they are gone, he says he can
now speak more freely than 'before hermits' pets'.

His references to honey are equally ambiguous.
He speaks of honey in his veins that makes his
soul quieter. And quietness is hardly a Nietzschean
virtue. Then he insists that, when he climbs the

mountain, he must take with him, 'yellow, white, fine, ice-cool golden honey'. (A phrase to set Pooh Bear's mouth watering!) He explains why he needs the honey: 'For I intend to make the honey offering.' Yet again when he is alone, he says, 'That I spoke of . . . honey offerings was merely a ruse . . .'

What are we to make of all this?

Who represents Zarathustra in the World of Pooh?
So far as Zarathustra's relations with the animals are concerned, one school of thought argues that this parallels Christopher Robin's relations with 'his' animals. They support their argument by pointing out that Christopher Robin is the only human character in Milne's book, just as Zarathustra is the only human character in the chapter we are discussing. They also argue that Christopher Robin's final withdrawal from the Forest parallels Zarathustra's withdrawal from his animal friends on the mountain top.

This is the sort of argument that sounds plausible when looked at in isolation, but falls to pieces as soon as we try to apply it to the facts it professes to explain. While it is true that Christopher Robin and Zarathustra are the only human characters in their respective groups, the contrasts between them are far deeper than this superficial similarity. Christopher Robin's intellectual limitations have been so amply demonstrated in earlier chapters that my readers will dismiss any attempt to identify him as the representative of Zarathustra. Detailed refutation is superfluous.

Though only the most obstinate will cling to the Christopher-Zarathustra hypothesis, others may challenge us to produce one more acceptable. Now while the simple refutation of other people's errors is perfectly legitimate – not to mention highly enjoyable – it is even better if we can replace them with a nearer approach to the truth, at least with something more consonant with the evidence.

The question confronting us at this moment is, who in the World of Pooh enacts the role of Zarathustra in this particular context? The answer, as every perceptive reader already intuitively knows, is the Great Bear himself. His massive intellectual superiority makes this obvious from the start. But we should not perhaps rely purely on this *a priori* argument. Nor need we. There is abundant empirical evidence in support.

For example, (1) Pooh Bear's oscillations between the solitude in which he lives and the society of the other Forest dwellers clearly replicate Zarathustra's oscillations between solitude and society. (2) Pooh climbs trees: Zarathustra climbs mountains. We note in passing that Pooh soaring above the earth in the balloon episode is the more triumphantly transcendent. (3) One of the many functions of Pooh's circular pursuit of the Woozle is to illustrate Nietzsche's strange doctrine of the Great Recurrence, the doctrine 'that all things recur eternally and we ourselves with them, and that we have already existed an infinite number of times before and all things with us.'

A fourth argument rests on Zarathustra's statement that honey was something that 'even grumbling bears . . . are greedy for'. How are we to interpret this? Our immediate reaction is that Pooh is certainly not a grumbling bear. Clearly therefore there can be no one-to-one relation between him and the grumbling bear. If we give, as we must, full weight to Nietzsche's 'even', we see the double purpose of this statement. The bear referred to is like Pooh in loving honey, but unlike him in being a grumbling bear. This clearly entails differentiating Pooh from grumbling bears and giving, or rather recognizing, his quite different status. As Nietzsche repeatedly celebrates joy and condemns grudging and grumbling, Pooh's status is not merely different: it is superior.

Thus it is undoubtedly Pooh himself who represents Zarathustra in this context. We may safely go further. This is one of several passages where Nietzsche implicitly but unmistakably recognizes Winnie-the-Pooh as a Superbear.

Having satisfactorily solved the problem of precisely how Pooh Bear relates to this chapter of *Thus Spake Zarathustra*, we move on to the problem of honey. The obvious Pooh reference is the episode of the Heffalump Trap.

'I have decided to catch a Heffalump.' Pooh follows up this declaration of intent by deciding to bait the Heffalump Trap with honey. We have already looked at this episode from several points of view. Now we approach it in the context of Nietzsche's references to honey in *Thus Spake Zarathustra*. At once we remember Zarathustra's statement that he desired honey as bait, and his rhetorical question, 'Have I not enticed him [the Higher Man] to me with honey offerings . . .?'

Eeyore and Nietzsche
We are introduced to Eeyore in the following words –

> The Old Grey Donkey, Eeyore, stood by himself in a thistly corner of the Forest, his front feet well apart, his head on one side, and thought about things. Sometimes he thought sadly to himself, 'Why?' and sometimes he thought, 'Wherefore?' and sometimes he thought, 'Inasmuch as which?' – and sometimes he didn't quite know what he *was* thinking about.

I suppose by now my readers have grown accustomed to the blindness of previous readers – Ursinian scholars and philosophers alike – to the philosophic depths of the World of Pooh. Yet surely they will be shocked to learn that, up to now, no one has commented on the glaringly obvious implications of this description; a description all the more significant because it is our first sight of Eeyore, and one, therefore, that must colour all our subsequent responses to him.

What then does it tell us? That he thinks about things. That he thinks sadly. That he asks 'Why?', 'Wherefore?', 'Inasmuch as which?' That he sometimes gets lost in the maze of his own questions. All this is a clear concrete realization of number 11 in the 'Maxims and Arrows' of Nietzsche's *Twilight of the Idols*, which runs,

> Can an *ass* be tragic? – To be crushed by a
> burden one can neither bear nor throw off? . . .
> The case of the philosopher.

There we have it all: the sadness; the specifically philosophical questions; their sometimes paralysing complexity.

Eeyore and the Ass Festival

Eeyore is enough of a philosopher to formulate major questions. Unlike Pooh Bear, he cannot answer them. This limited achievement indirectly reveals to us the high intellectual standard of even the lesser dwellers in the Forest. They demonstrate this in the last chapter of *Winnie-the-Pooh*. We all remember that

Christopher Robin gives a party to celebrate Pooh Bear's ingenuity and courage during the flood. We remember too that Eeyore mistakenly thinks the party is being given for him and tries to take it over. But the others ignore this attempt and continue to honour Pooh.

Compare this with the scene depicted in the chapters of *Thus Spake Zarathustra* entitled 'The Awakening' and 'The Ass Festival'. In the former, Zarathustra is amazed to find a group of men, including two kings, a retired pope, and a prophet, worshipping an ass. The ass responds to their litany of praise with a bray at the end of each clause. The likeness to Eeyore is pointed up by the worshippers' reference to his greyness and by their saying, 'A thistle titillates your heart.'

Though Zarathustra finds their worship absurd, in the end, he does not entirely condemn it. He regards their joyful worship of the ass as a step on the way to spiritual recovery. He tells them to remember the Ass Festival, and, if they repeat it, to do so for love of him.

Lovable though Eeyore is, can we imagine any of the others in the World of Pooh worshipping him? If they did, can we imagine anyone seeing it as a step towards spiritual health? A clear indication that, just as our Superbear surpasses the grumbling bear, so do the ordinary denizens of the Forest surpass the motley crew who inhabit Part Four of *Thus Spake Zarathustra*.

Some readers may feel that I have ignored the deepest element of this Part: the religious element. I am bound to agree with them. But examination of this element would take us into the realm of Natural Theology. While this may be regarded as a legitimate branch of philosophy, it does lie outside the main stream, which supplies quite enough material for a brief introductory work of this kind.

Nietzsche is often seen as one of the major forerunners of Existentialism, which is the subject of our next, and final, chapter.

7

Pooh and Existentialism

Existentialism: a label with many meanings
Martin Heidegger, Jean-Paul Sartre, Gabriel Marcel, Albert Camus are among the thinkers usually labelled 'Existentialist', though several of them rejected that label. And indeed they did disagree on many important points. However, they shared one vital characteristic: all of them produced interesting and often lengthy footnotes to certain particular aspects of Winnie-the-Pooh.

A note on time
Time is a key concept for many existentialists, especially for Martin Heidegger, whose longest work is entitled *Being and Time*. It is therefore appropriate

that it poses a certain problem in this chapter. We all know by now that most of Western philosophy leads up to Winnie-the-Pooh, who is its greatest expositor and critic. When, however, we come to philosophical works produced after 1926 (the date of *Winnie-the-Pooh*) and 1928 (the date of *The House at Pooh Corner*), we must consider them as footnotes to Ursinian wisdom.

To complicate matters, some of the philosophers we examine in this chapter published both before and after 1928. Others published about the same time. Heidegger's major work, for example, appeared in 1927 – exactly between Milne's two masterpieces: a fact we can hardly regard as merely accidental.

Where then should we draw the line between works which Pooh is expounding and works which are footnotes to Pooh? This must be a matter for my authorial decision.

Existentialists as footnotes to Pooh
Those familiar with existentialist thinkers will easily recognize Pooh's seminal influence on them. Conventional definitions of Existentialism emphasize such features as taking being rather than knowledge as the prime philosophical question; on concrete existence involving interaction with other existing beings, animate and inanimate; and the need to solve the problems of existence in relation

to experience rather than theory.

All of these are amply illustrated in the World of Pooh. Right at the beginning, we meet Pooh demonstrating the problem of Be(e)ing. There may be some who find it hard to take this argument quite seriously. But can we really doubt that the Milnean play on words inspired Heidegger's elaborate verbal analyses, often involving dubious etymologies? If any lurking doubt remains, it will be dispelled when we come to Heidegger's extended treatment of Pooh's analysis of thinking.

As for the existentialist emphasis on interaction with the world and solving the problems of actual existence, the whole World of Pooh is a varied and continuous illustration of this. Taking Pooh himself – and he is certainly not the only example – though he lives alone, he is no solitary thinker or detached observer. He is constantly with his friends in the Forest. He is concerned with such varied things as honey, finding Eeyore's tail, going on an Expotition, looking for a Woozle and rescuing Piglet.

Pooh and Gabriel Marcel (1889–1973)

When Christopher Robin is preparing for the Expotition to the North Pole, he tells Pooh,

'And we must all bring Provisions.'

'Bring what?'
'Things to eat.'
'Oh!' said Pooh happily. 'I thought you said
Provisions.'

This is just one of the passages that must have
inspired Gabriel Marcel to write,

> The dynamic element in my philosophy, taken
> as a whole, can be seen as an obstinate and
> untiring battle against the spirit of abstraction.

How powerfully Pooh exemplifies the struggle
against abstraction that Marcel proclaims! Note
Pooh's insistence that Christopher Robin translate
the general, abstract term 'provisions' into the concrete 'things to eat'. Note also that while Marcel
himself uses somewhat abstract language to describe
his struggle against abstraction, Pooh is practising
what he preaches.

This is not an isolated instance. We easily recall
how often and how vividly Pooh Bear illustrates the
fight against abstraction. He does not talk abstractly
about sweetness and light, or Truth, or the Absolute,
but concretely about honey and condensed milk
and marmalade. Nor does Pooh confine his preference for concrete particulars to inanimate objects.
Consider the following examples of practical benevolence:

Pooh and
Existentialism

1. Pooh tells Owl,

   '. . . Eeyore, who is a friend of mine, has lost
   his tail. And he's Moping about it. So could
   you very kindly tell me how to find it
   for him?'

2. Readers will remember the incident at the end
   of *The House at Pooh Corner*, when Eeyore, unwit-
   tingly and with the best intentions, presents Owl
   with Piglet's house.

   And then Piglet did a Noble Thing, and he
   did it in a sort of dream, while he was thinking
   of all the wonderful words Pooh had hummed
   about him.
      'Yes, it's just the house for Owl,' he said
   grandly. 'And I hope he'll be very happy in
   it.' And then he gulped twice, because he
   had been very happy in it himself.

   Then Christopher Robin asks where Piglet himself
   is going to live –

   Before Piglet could think, Pooh answered
   for him.
      'He'd come and live with me,' said Pooh,
   'wouldn't you, Piglet?'
      Piglet squeezed his paw.
      'Thank you, Pooh,' he said, 'I should love
   to.'

In these two instances, Pooh is not extolling a generalized benevolence: he is doing particular acts of kindness to particular persons. As for Piglet, in Professor John Macquarrie's words, 'he is both projecting and realizing an image of personhood'. The idea of realizing an image of personhood is underlined in the second of the above examples, when we are told that Piglet's generous gesture was stimulated by his desire to live up to the heroic image in Pooh's hum about him.

I chose these two examples because they had not been examined in previous chapters; but readers must be well aware that they do not stand alone. Eeyore's birthday, building a house for Eeyore, and rescuing Piglet from the flood – these spring readily to mind as concrete acts of kindness to specific persons. In all of them we see Pooh acting in the spirit of William Blake's dictum, 'He who would do good to another must do it in Minute Particulars.' And Blake has important affinities with Existentialism.

Pooh and Heidegger (1889–1976)

Perhaps I should preface this section by remarking that Heidegger is an extremely controversial figure. Some professionally competent judges rank him as the greatest philosopher of the twentieth century.

Others regard him as a pretentious charlatan. However this may be, he was, as I shall demonstrate, a profound student of the Great Bear, whose imprint may be found on almost every page of Heidegger's work. He therefore demands detailed attention in this chapter.

The familiar phrase 'the World of Pooh' itself signals a strong connection with Heidegger. The index to the English translation of *Being and Time* lists no fewer than one hundred and sixteen subdivisions of 'world'. This does not include a separate, and well-filled entry 'Being-in-the-world'. None of my readers can doubt that this demonstrates how thoroughly Heidegger had studied and meditated on the World of the Great Bear. If only he had followed his exemplar's clarity of style as well as his depth of thought!

Pooh's use of a balloon as a tool to get honey is obviously the key to Heidegger's emphasis on the use of tools and equipment to deal with the world outside. Even Heidegger's favourite phrase 'ready-to-hand' to indicate equipment clearly derives from Pooh's phrase 'about you', when he asks, 'I wonder if you've got such a thing as a balloon about you?'

Pooh, Heidegger and thinking

At a later stage of his interaction with the bees, Pooh says, 'I have just been thinking, and I have come to a very important decision. *These are the wrong sort of bees.'*

Our author's italics warn us to look for special importance. As the three statements in this Ursinian utterance inspired many pages of Heidegger, let us examine them one by one.

1. 'I have been thinking.' This clearly directs us to a late work of Heidegger entitled *What is Called Thinking?* You will all remember that the context of Pooh's remark is that he has just been stung by a bee. This gives a clear answer to what Heidegger called the decisive question: 'What is That which directs us into thinking?' In Pooh's case, the answer is simply: being stung by a bee.

No doubt it was this that made Heidegger realize that what directed him into thinking was the question of Be(e)ing. We might say, What stung him into thinking? A wrong concept of being. He was figuratively stung into realizing its wrongness, just as Pooh was stung literally – though symbolically too – into the same realization. Can we doubt that Heidegger seized on this punning reference and made it the basis of a large area of his thought?

2. 'I have come to a decision.' 'Decision' means the same as Heidegger's favourite term 'resoluteness'. This interpretation is further supported when we remember that Pooh says these words when he is

still airborne with his balloon but very shortly before he returns to earth. Heidegger referred to this when he said, 'Resoluteness does not detach [the authentic self] from its world, nor does it isolate it so that it becomes a free-floating "I".' The combination of resolute decision with acted-out rejection of a free-floating 'I' puts it beyond all reasonable doubt that Heidegger was commenting on this very passage.

3. *'These are the wrong sort of bees.'* Pooh goes on to say these wrong bees would make the wrong sort of honey. We can see that Heidegger built the whole vast edifice of *Being and Time* on his insight that Pooh's rejection of the wrong sort of bees indicated that a wrong concept of being would produce a false philosophy instead of the genuine honey of truth and wisdom.

Pooh, Heidegger and language

Pooh tells us, 'Poetry and Hums aren't things which you get, they're things which get *you*.' Heidegger generalized this when he wrote, 'Language speaks.' Let us examine a more elaborate example.

> At breakfast . . . he had suddenly thought of a new song. It began like this:

>> *'Sing Ho! for the life of a Bear.'*

When he had got as far as this, he scratched
his head, and thought to himself, 'That's a very
good start for a song, but what about the second
line?' He tried singing 'Ho,' two or three times,
but it didn't seem to help. 'Perhaps it would be
better,' he thought, 'if I sang Hi for the life of a
Bear.' So he sang it . . . but it wasn't.

Heidegger's commentary, in 'The Nature of language', goes as follows:

But when the issue is to put into language
something which has never yet been spoken,
then everything depends on whether language
gives or withholds the appropriate word. Such
is the case of the poet.

The substitution of 'Hi' proves unsatisfactory.

'Very well, then,' he [Pooh] said, 'I shall sing
that first line twice, and perhaps if I sing it very
quickly, I shall find myself singing the third and
fourth lines before I have time to think of them,
and that will be a Good Song.'

Just as these lines continue the previous quotation
from Pooh, so the previous quotation from Heidegger
goes on, 'Indeed, a poet might even come to the
point where he is compelled – in his own way, that
is, poetically – to put into language the experience

he undergoes with language.' Even more strikingly, Heidegger goes on, 'The song is sung, not after it has come to be, but rather: in the singing the song begins to be a song.'

This clearly refers to the moment when Pooh triumphantly achieves his Good Song. As a parallel, Heidegger quotes Stefan George's poem 'The Word'. Of course, we cannot help noticing Pooh's superiority: he creates his own poetic example, whereas Heidegger is driven to quote someone else's.

As Heidegger's essay was published in 1959, we must congratulate him on having produced one of the most striking footnotes to Winnie-the-Pooh.

Pooh, Heidegger and the Expotition to the North Pole
The Expotition to the North Pole is particularly rich in influences on Heidegger. We have already noted the deep relevance of Pooh's Good Song, which opens the chapter. Then the Expotition itself begins 'at the top of the Forest', and all set off through the country. We already know that the North Pole represents, among other things, philosophic truth, so we have no difficulty in seeing that this Expotition was in Heidegger's mind when he wrote, 'Thinking abides in that country, walking the ways of that country.'

While walking the ways of that country, Pooh and his friends pass a Dangerous Place. It would be

easy to dismiss this as a warning against the dangers
that lie in wait for the unwary thinker. Doubtless that
meaning is there, but surely we know enough by
now to suspect something deeper. As always with
Winnie-the-Pooh, we soon find what we are looking
for.

> They came to a place where the banks widened
> out at each side, so that on each side of the
> water there was a level strip of grass on which
> they could sit down and rest.

This is obviously Heidegger's 'openness as a region
. . . which permits . . . an expanded resting'.

'All this is very well,' hasty readers may say, 'but
what has it to do with the Dangerous Place?' Have
patience and all will be revealed.

Christopher Robin explains that the Place is Dangerous because –

> 'It's just the place [. . .] for an Ambush.'
>   'What sort of bush?' whispered Pooh to Piglet.
> 'A gorse-bush?'

Owl explains an Ambush is a sort of Surprise.

> 'So is a gorse-bush sometimes,' said Pooh.

'Pooh . . . said that a gorse-bush had sprung at him

suddenly one day when he fell off a tree, and he had taken six days to get all the prickles out of himself.' The obvious Heideggerian reference is 'we take the region itself as that which comes to meet us.' How brilliantly the gorse-bush springing at Pooh enacts the somewhat obscure notion of a region coming to meet us!

Omitting several other references, we come to the climax of this chapter: the finding of the North Pole.

> Pooh looked at the pole in his hands.
> 'I just found it,' he said. 'I thought it ought to be useful. I just picked it up.' [More references to ready-to-handness and equipment.]
> 'Pooh,' said Christopher Robin solemnly, 'the

Expedition is over. You have found the North
Pole!'

This is undoubtedly Christopher Robin's moment
of triumph. Though Pooh found the pole, it is
Christopher Robin who names it the North Pole. We
cannot fail to remember Heidegger's 'To assign the
naming word is, after all, what constitutes finding.'

This incident may puzzle some readers. Can we
believe, they may wonder, that the true finder was
that well-meaning but dim-witted boy? Was he, even
for once, ahead of the Great Bear? If we can swallow
this massive improbability, why then did Pooh go
home 'feeling very proud of himself'?

The more perceptive readers will have understood
the true meaning of this incident. Winnie-the-Pooh
had led Christopher Robin to the correct answer
by showing him the pole (lower case 'p'). In the
context of the search, he hoped that Christopher
Robin would recognize that it was the Pole (upper
case 'P'). For once, he was not disappointed. It was
his success as a teacher of very unpromising material
that made Pooh – rightly – very proud. Incidentally,
the distinction between 'pole' and 'Pole' of course
led Heidegger to his key distinction between 'being'
and 'Being'.

Alas! Christopher Robin did not live up to this
moment of promise. At the very end, we see him
proudly displaying an incoherent collection of unco-

ordinated facts as proof he was being educated; and then leaving the Forest. Heidegger was fond of paths as a metaphor. In this sense, leaving the Forest means taking one of the paths that lead out of philosophy altogether. Just as well, perhaps, as Christopher Robin certainly had no aptitude for it.

Pooh and the call of the twelve pots of honey
When Rabbit's typically unsuccessful attempt to unbounce Tigger ends in the unbouncers getting lost, Pooh says,

> 'Now then, Piglet, let's go home.'
> 'But, Pooh,' cried Piglet, all excited, 'do
> you know the way?'
> 'No,' said Pooh. 'But there are twelve pots
> of honey in my cupboard, and they've been
> calling to me for hours. I couldn't hear them
> properly before, because Rabbit *would* talk, but
> if nobody says anything except those twelve
> pots, I *think*, Piglet, I shall know where they're
> calling from.'

Here Pooh shows us with perfect clearness what it means to listen to the voice of being – in this case, to the being of the pots of honey. As scholars, we are only too familiar with footnotes that confuse rather than elucidate the text they profess to explain.

We must confess that Heidegger's annotations of this passage are a painful example of this. To talk of openness to Being as something that 'implies circumspective concern, and has the character of being affected in some way' is an excessively ponderous way of telling us what Milne has already told us far more clearly: that Pooh was looking around him (being circumspective, in Heidegger's terms), was concerned, both with the honey and with finding the way home, and was affected by both.

Still, we cannot doubt Heidegger was trying to comment on Pooh, especially when we remember he also talked of 'the hearing which understands'; a kind of hearing Pooh so eminently displays on this occasion. We find yet further proof of this when Pooh tells Piglet he could not hear the honey-pots before, because Rabbit kept talking. Heidegger commented briefly on the obstructive power of chatter when he wrote, 'by its very nature, idle talk is a closing-off.'

Rabbit's endless attempts at superficially methodical thought drew Heidegger's comment, 'Calculative thinking never stops, never collects itself . . . meditative thinking . . . contemplates the meaning which reigns in everything that is.' Heidegger is often obscure, but we must congratulate him on this brilliant thumbnail sketch of Rabbit.

Heidegger and the end of 'Pooh'

All Ursinians will agree that the only thing that makes the end of *The House at Pooh Corner* bearable is the knowledge, based on repeated experience, that the books are infinitely rereadable. The last chapter is called 'The Enchanted Place'. The last words are 'So they went off together. But wherever they go, and whatever happens to them on the way, in that enchanted place on the top of the Forest a little boy and his Bear will always be playing.' Who can read this without seeing how obviously it is the text on which Heidegger commented when he wrote of 'an enchanted region where everything belonging there returns to that in which it rests'?

Heidegger is generally regarded as the greatest of those given the existentialist label; a label he himself rejected. However, he was comparatively little known, and less read, by those for whom 'existentialism' became a cult-word in the 1950s and 60s. For these, being an existentialist consisted of wearing black jeans and black polo-necks, and talking about one's *angst* (a generalized feeling of dread without any particular object) and authentic living. If existentialists of this sort had been asked to name an existentialist philosopher, most would have named Jean-Paul Sartre, to whom we now turn.

Jean-Paul Sartre (1905–80)

Sartre's fame was due partly to his political activity;
partly to his success as a novelist and dramatist. He
was, in fact, a far better novelist and dramatist than
he was a philosopher. Indeed, the most impressive
passages in his major philosophical work, *Being and
Nothingness*, are vividly dramatic portrayals of specific events, which might well have appeared in one of
his novels or plays.

Pooh, *'Being and Nothingness'*

Being and Nothingness is the title of Sartre's major
philosophical work. As it first appeared in 1943
(682 pages of text in the original French; 626 larger
pages in Hazel Barnes's English translation), we must
consider it the longest single footnote to Winnie-the-
Pooh ever written.

Can we doubt that Sartre's key concept of Nothingness was derived from Chapter Three of *The House
at Pooh Corner*? The text which reads, 'Pooh . . .
stepped on a piece of the Forest which had been
left out by mistake,' clearly led Sartre to comment,
'emptiness is emptiness *of* something': Pooh experi-
ences the emptiness by falling into the pit caused
by the emptiness where there should have been a
piece of the Forest. Pooh's judgment that he has
fallen comes after and as a result of the absence

of a piece of the Forest, and so enacts Sartre's more abstract statement that 'the negative judgment (there was not a piece of the forest there) . . . is conditioned and supported by non-being.'

When Christopher Robin asks Piglet what the Heffalump looked like, Piglet answered, '– like an enormous big nothing'. When Eeyore tells Christopher Robin his house has disappeared, the two of them go off together and soon come to the place 'where Eeyore's house wasn't . . .'.

After these brief passing references to the problem of nothingness, we find Pooh Bear meeting it head on.

On the first page of *The House at Pooh Corner*, Pooh goes 'round to Piglet's house to see what Piglet was doing'. On arrival, he finds he cannot do this, because 'the more he looked inside the more Piglet wasn't there.'

This will remind all who have read even the first few pages of *Being and Nothingness* of Sartre's anecdote of going to a café to keep an appointment with Pierre and discovering Pierre is not there. As he puts it, 'Pierre absent haunts this cafe . . .' Not a bad equivalent for Milne's 'the more he looked inside the more Piglet wasn't there', though lacking the vivid concreteness of the great original.

This, of course, is typical of scholarly footnotes. So is the length of Sartre's footnote: it covers just over a page and a half; Milne says it all in a short paragraph.

A passage near the end of *The House at Pooh Corner* seems to have profoundly influenced Sartre.

> [Christopher Robin said] '. . . what I like *doing* best is Nothing.'
> 'How do you do Nothing?' asked Pooh, after he had wondered for a long time.
> 'Well, it's when people call out at you just as you're going off to do it, "What are you going to do, Christopher Robin?" and you say "Oh, nothing," and then you go and do it.'
> 'Oh, I see,' said Pooh.
> 'This is a nothing sort of thing we're doing now.'
> 'Oh, I see,' said Pooh again.
> 'It means just going along, listening to all the things you can't hear, and not bothering.'

I do not wish to be censorious – though it is always a pleasure – but I feel bound to say that it is a mark of Sartre's inferiority as a philosopher that this is the passage that most deeply affected his thinking. To spend over six hundred pages elaborating on a topic that the Great Bear took in his stride, and that even Christopher Robin was able to expound in a few sentences, is painful evidence of secondrateness. It might have been better if he had paid more attention to Christopher Robin's last words and not bothered.

Nevertheless, we must admit Sartre's power as a dramatist. His *Huis Clos*, for example, is set in a very convincing modern hell. The traditional physical torments are not needed there, because the three main characters are doomed to torture each other emotionally and psychologically, for ever.

How can we connect this horrific vision with the sunny world of Pooh? What is there in common between the three mutual tormentors of *Huis Clos* and the friendly, co-operative World of Pooh? Between the claustrophobic Second Empire room that imprisons the damned trio and the spacious Forest where Pooh and his friends roam at will?

One obvious solution is to invoke Sartre's concept of Nothingness as intervening between subject and object and separating them. According to this interpretation, Nothingness would separate Sartre as subject from the World of Pooh as object. Thus separated, Sartre was bound to interpret the text in the light of his own preoccupation with *angst* and nausea.

Attractive though this explanation is, my readers may find it perhaps a little forced. I am inclined to agree. As the last thing I wish to do is to present any explanation that does not arise obviously and inevitably out of the text, I must look further.

In this case, I am inclined to look at *Huis Clos* less as a footnote in the formal sense than as a creative work in its own right, yet one clearly dependent on Winnie-the-Pooh for its inspiration. This allows us to recognize Sartre's dramatic genius while perceiving a new aspect of the great text we are studying: its power of inspiring major works by other writers. Once again we must marvel at its extraordinary richness. How many works have inspired a great drama with one short paragraph?

The relationship just established between Pooh and Sartre is particularly appropriate, since both combined philosophy with literature: Pooh as poet; Sartre as novelist and dramatist.

Pooh, 'angst', bad faith, and authenticity

This would seem an appropriate place to deal with a question which may have been lurking in my readers' minds as this chapter has gone on. The question of how Pooh deals with *angst* and nausea. '*Angst*' is a common term in much existentialist writing; 'nausea' is particularly characteristic of Sartre; it is indeed the title of one of his novels. Nor is this accidental or peripheral. All existentialists emphasize that human existence is stressful, and that we must confront this stress. Only by confronting and making free choices in the face of it do we live authentically. To evade or ignore it is to be in a state of bad faith. So is denying our responsibility for our choices. Given these facts about existentialism, the question is, where are the connections with the World of Pooh?

There are several possible answers to this. 1. We may take this aspect of existentialism as a hostile

critique of the World of Pooh. Existentialists may
be saying that this world is precisely a world of
bad faith, of cowardly evasion. 2. We may extend
our interpretation of *Huis Clos* to other existentialist
texts, and regard them as inspired by Milne rather
than as footnotes to or commentaries on him. 3. We
may regard them as expansions of themes treated
briefly in Milne. As so often, we shall find the 'both-
and' approach more fruitful than the 'either-or'. In
other words, we shall find that all three answers
are applicable in part, and we may even find an
ultimate synthesis. So let us take each in turn, and
then explore the possibility of combining them.

1.   'Tigger is all right, *really*,' said Piglet lazily.
     'Of course he is,' said Christopher Robin.
     'Everybody is *really*,' said Pooh. 'That's what
I think,' said Pooh. 'But I don't suppose I'm
right,' he said.
     'Of course you are,' said Christopher Robin.

It would be hard to find a more emphatic contradiction of 'Hell is other people', Sartre's famous
statement at the end of *Huis Clos*. Surely this short
passage encapsulates all that the author of *Huis Clos*
and *Nausea* would find optimistically evasive of harsh
reality in the World of Pooh.

In Chapter Six of *The House at Pooh Corner*, Rabbit
asks Eeyore, who has just emerged from the river,

'How did you fall in, Eeyore?' . . .
'I didn't,' said Eeyore.
'But how –'
'I was BOUNCED,' said Eeyore.

Rabbit suspects Tigger was the Bouncer – reasonably enough, as Tigger is Bouncy by nature. Tigger at first denies having bounced Eeyore. Step by step he comes nearer to confessing: 'I didn't really. I had a cough, and I happened to be behind Eeyore, and I said *"Grrrr–oppp–ptschschschz."* ' Then, crossly 'I didn't bounce, I coughed.' Finally, he admits 'Well, I sort of boffed.'

So now we have clear examples of two sorts of lack of authenticity of a specially Sartrean kind: evasion of reality, and evasion of personal responsibility. These examples came from individual characters in particular situations; but look at this:

But, of course, it isn't really Good-bye, because the Forest will always be there . . . and anybody who is Friendly with Bears can find it.

. . . in that enchanted place on the top of the Forest, a little boy and his Bear will always be playing.

Both these statements were made by the author directly, in his own voice. Their placing, at the

---

beginning and end of *The House at Pooh Corner* gives them very special weight.

So far the case for a hostile existentialist critique seems strong. Let us, however suspend judgment while we examine the other possible interpretations.

2. The suggestion that *Winnie-the-Pooh* and *The House at Pooh Corner* served the existentialists as a source of inspiration rather than as texts for commentary and explication obviously has much to commend it, but by its very nature – general rather than specific – it is difficult to support convincingly in such a brief and elementary work as this. A few references must suffice. Interested readers can follow them up for themselves.

Roo has not so far played any part in our exposition, but now his time has come. One of the things we remember most clearly about him is his Strengthening Medicine. 'He hates it,' Piglet tells us. And what is it? Extract of Malt. And what adjective leaps to mind to describe Extract of Malt? 'Viscous.' The reference to a viscous substance which produces nausea in Roo is undoubtedly the source of Sartre's *Nausea*. Perusal of that excellent novel will both convince and reward those who read it.

'Winnie-the-Pooh came stumping along' and noticed Eeyore's tail was missing. After some conversation on the subject,

---

Pooh felt that he ought to say something helpful
about it, but didn't quite know what. So he
decided to do something helpful instead.
    'Eeyore,' he said solemnly, 'I, Winnie-the-
Pooh, will find your tail for you.'

Let us ponder this scene a little. Pooh comes 'stumping' through the Forest. Milne's Flaubertian precision
in choosing the *mot juste* makes it clear that the Bear
was not wandering or strolling but proceeding with
firm purpose, something that implies a previous
decision. Yet when he learns of Eeyore's distress,
he quickly and resolutely makes a new decision.
First, he considers helpful words, but realizes in
a flash that no words could be adequate to the
situation; for what words could restore Eeyore's
tail? Immediately, he resolves on action; and he
acts.

Sartre must have remembered this when he gave
the lecture translated into English under the title
of *Existentialism and Humanism*. This, you remember, contains the anecdote of the young man who
came to Sartre during the Second World War,
asking the philosopher how he should solve his
problem: whether to stay to support his widowed
mother in France or go to England to join the Free
French forces under General de Gaulle. The parallel
is unmistakable, but perhaps it is worthwhile filling
in a few details.

Pooh's determined and purposeful approach

strongly suggests he was embarking on a journey of some length: something equivalent, in other words, to the young Frenchman's embarking for England. At this stage, there was no dilemma for Pooh for no other choice presented itself as a moral obligation. This occurred only when he learned of Eeyore's distressing loss. Unlike Sartre's young acquaintance, Pooh does not seek advice about what he should do, but makes his existential choice in full and responsible freedom. Thus he attains the authenticity that Sartre tried to enforce by compelling the young man to choose for himself.

3. Now we come to the third solution. This sees some existentialist writing as an expansion of themes only touched on in the *Pooh* books. To examine this, we must return to the passages we looked at under our first heading, but now we must analyse them more closely.

Our first example was the discussion of Tigger by, in order of speaking, Piglet, Pooh Bear, Christopher Robin. On our first reading, we were content to accept the most obvious meaning. Now we analyse the short dialogue into the following propositions:

1. It is the case that Tigger is really all right. (Piglet)
2. It is the case that, as a matter of course, Tigger is all right. (Christopher Robin)
3. It is the case that everybody is all right. (Pooh)

4. It is the case that Pooh thinks that everyone is all right. (Pooh)
5. It is the case that Pooh does not think it is the case that he is right in thinking it is the case that everybody is all right. (Pooh)
6. It is the case that Pooh is right. (Christopher Robin)

Propositions 1, 2 and 6 are, on the whole, fairly straightforward. Some Ursinian scholars have found ambiguity in 6, arguing that Christopher Robin's statement might mean either (a) that Pooh was correct in thinking everybody was all right really, or (b) that Pooh was correct in supposing this judgment was erroneous. I must say I find interpretation (b) intuitively implausible. It credits Christopher Robin with a subtlety quite outside his range.

We may agree, therefore, that we can take the statement by Piglet and both statements by Christopher Robin at their face value, though what that is we must consider later. Now for the crux of the matter: the three profoundly problematical statements of the Great Bear himself (equivalent to 3, 4 and 5 in our list of propositions).

Three and four are both straightforward assertions. The fifth is far less confident in tone. The key question is how we are to interpret Pooh's last statement and its relation to his first and second. By now, I trust it would be superfluous to warn my readers against taking it as expressing the properly modest self-doubt of a Bear of Very Little Brain. The absurdity of such an interpretation has been amply and repeatedly proved. But what interpretation shall we offer in its place?

If for a moment we may stray into the realm of psychology, we remember that a philosophically-minded psychologist, Professor Michael Billig, believes that thought is a kind of argument with oneself. Clearly this is what Pooh is doing in this instance. In more philosophical terms, he is thinking dialectically. Should anyone object that this is Hegelian rather than existentialist, the answer is that Sartre was deeply influenced by Hegelianism, both in its original and its Marxist form. So we may rest assured that Sartre's *Huis Clos*, with its powerfully demonstrated 'Hell is other people', is, from our point of view, simply the dramatic elaboration of the negative pole of Pooh's thought on this occasion.

This conclusion is strongly supported by the sharp contrast between the depth and complexity of Pooh's statements and the characteristically simple and superficial statements of Piglet and Christopher Robin. They indeed may be criticized for an excessively rosy picture of the world. Pooh himself is clearly aware of its dark underside, though he left the detailed exploration of it to the existentialists. That, in fact, puts it too weakly: the preceding pages have shown he inspired their exploration.

Much the same applies to the treatment of authenticity and bad faith. When we look back at Tigger's response to the charge of BOUNCING Eeyore, we note his prolonged effort to avoid authentic responsibility for his own choice. First he tries flat denial. When that fails, he tries that characteristic form of bad faith: placing the responsibility for his action on something he claims he could not control: in this case, his cough. The moral confusion of bad faith is superbly summarized in the nonce-word 'boffed'.

We cannot doubt that Sartre had this passage in mind when he wrote, 'The existentialist does not believe in the power of passion. He will never regard a grand passion as a destructive torrent upon which a man is swept into certain actions as by fate, and which, therefore, is an excuse for them. He thinks that man is responsible for his passion.' Sartre is here exploring coughing as a metaphor for passion; a peculiarly appropriate metaphor when we remember that coughing is metonymically related to sneezing, which in turn is sometimes a metaphor for the male orgasm.

Piglet and existential choice

> 'It is hard to be brave,' said Piglet, sniffing
> slightly, 'when you're only a Very Small
> Animal.'

Though Piglet expressed fear of Kanga because he had heard 'that a Kanga was Generally Regarded as One of the Fiercer Animals' and was doubly fierce when 'Deprived of Its Young', yet when he was told he was essential to Rabbit's plan, 'he forgot to be frightened any more . . .'

When Pooh celebrated Piglet's heroism in the rescue of Wol, he wrote,

> O gallant Piglet (PIGLET)! Ho!
>   Did Piglet tremble? Did he blinch?
>   No, No, he struggled inch by inch
> Through LETTERS ONLY, as I know
> Because I saw him go.

When Pooh sings this song, Piglet says, '. . . I – I thought I did blinch a little. Just at first. And it says, "Did he blinch no no." '

'You only blinched inside,' said Pooh, 'and
that's the bravest way for a Very Small Animal
not to blinch that there is.'
Piglet sighed with happiness, and began to
think about himself. He was BRAVE . . .

Sartre's comments on this put into abstract terms
what Milne shows us in existential reality. Sartre
says, 'There are nervous temperaments; there is
what is called impoverished blood, and there are
also rich temperaments. But the man whose blood is
poor is not a coward for all that, for what produces
cowardice is the act of giving up or giving way; and
a temperament is not an action . . . the existentialist
says that the coward makes himself cowardly, the
hero makes himself heroic . . .' What better description could there be of Piglet, rising above his natural
timidity to act as a hero?

Pooh and Camus (1913–60)

The everyday man does not enjoy tarrying.
(Camus)

The sun was so delightfully warm, and the
stone, which had been sitting in it for a long
time, was so warm, too, that Pooh had almost
decided to go on being Pooh in the middle of
the stream for the rest of the morning.

Readers familiar with the work of Camus may feel
that I chose a very untypical quotation from *The
Myth of Sisyphus* for the beginning of this section.
The remark that the everyday man does not enjoy
tarrying, especially when paired with the description
of Pooh sitting on a sun-warmed stone, suggests a
recommendation of tranquillity. And tranquillity is
most uncharacteristic of a book that opens with
the famous sentence, 'There is but one truly serious
philosophical problem and that is suicide.'

I would justify my choice by arguing that Pooh's
influence on Camus was chiefly by way of contrast.

The pain and absurdity of the world of Camus was, as we shall see, his reaction to the happy world of Pooh. As the whole connection between Pooh and Camus has been scandalously neglected by experts in both fields, my readers may reasonably expect some evidence. This I shall be happy to give.

First, let us confront what is perhaps Camus's key concept: the Absurd. To him, this was the inescapable condition of human life.

We can agree that the Camus quotation recognizes that Pooh is not an Everyday Bear. Neither is he an Absurd Bear. The reason is easy to see. Camus tells us 'The Absurd is born of this confrontation between the human need and the unreasonable silence of the world.' But the World of Pooh is far from silent.

In the first few pages Pooh himself hears a loud buzzing-noise. Later, Eeyore hears a crackling in the bracken. Piglet hears a loud squawk from Owl. All the streams of the Forest tinkle. Cuckoos try their voices. Wood-pigeons complain gently. These are just some examples, carefully chosen at random from *Winnie-the-Pooh*. We notice also that these are not mere sounds: they mean something to those who hear them. So the basic conditions of the Absurd simply do not exist in the World of Pooh.

We can hardly avoid the conclusion that Camus' concept of the Absurd and his bitter picture of life in this world arose from his keen awareness of how different it was from the World of Pooh. In other words, his work was driven by his consciousness of the gulf between the two worlds. Once we realize this, we must acknowledge how fundamentally the Great Bear influenced Camus.

Camus himself implicitly acknowledges his debt when he writes, 'The irrational, the human nostalgia, and the absurd that is born of their encounter . . .' Does not this tell us plainly that his Absurd world is born of his nostalgia for the world of Pooh? And he recurs to this theme when he says, 'If I were a tree among trees, a cat among animals, this life would have a meaning or rather this problem [life's meaninglessness] would not arise, for I should belong to this world.' How sad is his envy for Pooh and his friends, all belonging to their world!

There were, though, a few places where he could make contact with Pooh. There was the occasion, early in *Winnie-the-Pooh*, when Pooh visits Rabbit, who regales him on honey and condensed milk. You remember what follows when he tries to leave.

> So he started to climb out of the hole. He
> pulled with his front paws, and pushed with
> his back paws, and in a little while his nose
> was out in the open again . . . and then his
> ears . . . and then his front paws . . . and then
> his shoulders . . . and then –
> 'Oh, help!' said Pooh. 'I'd better go back.'
> 'Oh, bother!' said Pooh. 'I shall have to go on.'

'I can't do either!' said Pooh. 'Oh, help
and bother!'

Lovers of Pooh will remember the rest of the saga
of the 'Wedged Bear in Great Tightness', but they
may not all be aware of Camus' comment: 'What I
touch, what resists me – that I understand.'

It is, perhaps typical that Camus should have
chosen to comment on an episode where Pooh
approaches as near as his nature permits to the
absurd, but he also commented on a happier incident; one which we have already examined in other
connections: the episode of the Wolery. Our last look
at it was so recent we need do no more than remark
how apposite was Camus' tribute to the generosity of
Piglet and Pooh. 'Real generosity towards the future,'
he wrote, 'lies in giving all to the present.'

Last words on Pooh and the existentialists
With Camus, we come to the end of our examination
of Pooh's influence on the existentialists, and of their
responses to him. Their often exaggerated emphasis
on the grimmer aspects of life were sometimes a
reaction against the well-balanced world of Pooh,
in others a somewhat one-sided elaboration of those
passages that show how well Milne understood both
the concept and the reality of *angst*.

Should anyone doubt his understanding, let us remember the scene when Piglet finds himself surrounded by water. ' "It's a little Anxious," he said to himself, "to be a Very Small Animal Entirely Surrounded by Water." ' Milne has given us a clear signal by capitalizing 'Anxious'. More, he has capitalized nearly all the rest of Piglet's sentence; a device that in this context must remind us of Heidegger. Nor does he leave it at that. He spells out the apparent hopelessness of Piglet's situation.

> 'Christopher Robin and Pooh could escape by
> Climbing Trees, and Kanga could escape by
> Jumping, and Rabbit could escape by Burrow-
> ing, and Owl could escape by Flying, and
> Eeyore could escape by – by Making a Loud
> Noise Until Rescued, and here am I, sur-
> rounded by water and I can't do *anything*.'

Could there be a more striking picture of the Being-towards-Death that Heidegger said was essential to authentic living?

Where, of course, Milne showed a greater breadth and depth was in showing Piglet not only facing the abyss of imminent destruction, in full existential authenticity, but transcending it by resolute – and intelligent – action. He wrote an appeal for help, and sent it off in a bottle. Then came the second stage, a stage where Piglet's message (or 'missage') was received and acted on by Pooh and Christopher Robin. Here we see how the World of Pooh was a world of social ties and personal friendship leading to co-operative action.

Existentialists have often been criticized for excessive individualism, for ignoring the social element in life. This is not entirely fair. But they would not have been open to the accusation if they had fully absorbed the lessons of the flood episode. For here they should have seen how to combine a powerful realization of individual *angst* with an equally powerful realization of the positive value of society.

Profound and stimulating thinkers though many of them were, they comprehended only a fraction of the Enormous Brain of Winnie-the-Pooh.

Tailpiece
(not Eeyore's)

I should not like the last sentence of the last chapter to be taken as singling out the existentialists for particular criticism. Now that we have come to the end of this brief and elementary introduction to philosophy in the World of Pooh, it must be abundantly clear that no other philosopher, no group of philosophers, has cultivated more than a small area of that world. From the earliest Greek cosmologists to the various schools that dominated the first half of this century, we have seen that the Great Bear contains them all.

What, you may ask, of those I have omitted? What about that vast area separating the Stoics and Epicureans from the seventeenth-century Rationalists? What about Plotinus, St Augustine of Hippo, Scotus

Erigena, Abelard, Aquinas, Duns Scotus and William of Ockham? Moving forward, what about those philosophers still alive – ranging from the absolute idealism of Timothy Sprigge to the physicalism of Patricia Smith Churchland, and including Philippa Foot and Elizabeth Anscombe, Bernard Williams and Stuart Hampshire, Daniel Dennett and Michael Lockwood, Jonathan Barnes, Hilary Putnam and W. H. Newton-Smith, John Searle and John Rawls, Ted Honderich, Willard van Orman Quine and Anthony Kenny – to name but a few?

Much as I sympathize with this objection, I think it overlooks the fact that this little book is addressed to the general reader, and therefore it is confined to those philosophers whose names at least are widely familiar. Thus, all readers of Wodehouse know that Jeeves was a devotee of Spinoza, and that he condemned Nietzsche as 'fundamentally unsound'. One could hardly claim an equal currency for the great philosophers of the Dark and Middle Ages.

Similarly with contemporary philosophers. Their contributions to the elaboration and elucidation of the Milnean opus would certainly call for detailed analysis if I were addressing professional philosophers. All I would say on that score is that I hope that any of them who do glance at this book may be encouraged to undertake a renewed, and more perceptive, study of the world of Pooh. I am sure they would benefit by it.

So, I hope, will others. It is sad to reflect on the length of time that has elapsed between the publication of *Winnie-the-Pooh* and the recognition of its scholarly importance.

As we should expect, Winnie-the-Pooh himself puts it in perspective. He clearly foresaw the gradual emergence of his intellectual reputation when he invented the game of Poohsticks. Rabbit saw the point, when he said, 'They [previous Ursinian scholars] always take longer than you think.'

We may be surprised that it was Rabbit who achieved this insight, but, as Eeyore said a little later, 'Give Rabbit time, and he'll always get the answer.' If Rabbit can, we can.

Pooh and the Magicians

John Tyerman Williams

With original line drawings by E.H. Shepard

Pooh and the Magicians reveals Winnie-the-Pooh as master of ancient lore. John Tyerman Williams explores A. A. Milne's classic stories, *Winnie-the-Pooh* and *The House at Pooh Corner,* to reveal fascinating hidden references to astrology, alchemy, hermetic philosophy, the Tarot, the Druids, I Ching, the Qabalah, and finally, the Female Mysteries which light the way to a Utopian society.

John Tyerman Williams proved in *Pooh and the Philosophers* that the whole of Western philosophy may be found in the stories of Winnie-the-Pooh. Now he goes further to reveal the hermetic tradition sealed inside a honey jar.

John Tyerman Williams is a Doctor of Philosophy and a former actor and lecturer on theatre, English history and English literature. He lives in Tintagel, Cornwall, close to the birthplace of the Arthurian Legends.

Pooh and the Psychologists

John Tyerman Williams

With original line drawings by E.H. Shepard

'...Winnie-the-Pooh lived in the forest all by himself under the name of Sanders,' and he had the name over the door in gold letters. Why 'Sanders'? And why gold letters?
Might not the gold letters stand for the brass plate of a physician, or a psychotherapist? Would the bell inform Pooh that a patient was waiting for his attention?

Discover the answers to John Tyerman Williams' hypothesis that Winnie-the-Pooh is a master of psychology and a brilliant psychotherapist in this humorous and searching exposé.

The Tao of Pooh

Benjamin Hoff

With original line drawings by E.H. Shepard

The Tao of Pooh has become a classic philosophical study of Winnie-the-Pooh. Winnie-the-Pooh has a certain way about him, a way of doing things which has made him the world's most beloved bear. And Pooh's Way, as Benjamin Hoff brilliantly demonstrates, seems strangely close to the ancient Chinese principles of Taoism.

While Eeyore frets ... and Piglet hesitates ... and Owl pontificates ... Pooh just is.

With examples from A. A. Milne's immensely popular classics, *Winnie-the-Pooh* and *The House at Pooh Corner*, Benjamin Hoff explains the principles of Taoist philosophy.

Benjamin Hoff is a writer, photographer, musician and composer, and a specialist in Japanese fine-pruning, with a degree in Asian Art. He writes full-time. In his spare time he practises Taoist yoga and T'ai Chi Ch'uan.
He lives in Portland, Oregon.

The Te of Piglet

Benjamin Hoff

With original line drawings by E.H. Shepard

In this sequel to *The Tao of Pooh*, author Benjamin Hoff explores the Te (a Chinese word meaning Virtue) of the Small – a principle embodied perfectly in Piglet. As delightful as it is instructive, *The Te of Piglet* features dialogues between the author and the familiar characters of Pooh, Eeyore, Tigger, Kanga and Baby Roo, and of course, Piglet himself. These conversations are interspersed with traditional Taoist stories and more than 50 illustrations from the original Pooh books.

Combining the irresistible charm of A. A. Milne's classic stories, the enduring wisdom of the ancient teachings, and the unique contemporary appeal of its predecessor, *The Tao of Pooh*, this book is sure to captivate the legions of readers who have found enlightenment and pleasure in walking in the Path of Pooh.

Benjamin Hoff is a writer, photographer, musician and composer, and a specialist in Japanese fine-pruning, with a degree in Ancient Art. He writes full-time. In his spare time he practises Taoist yoga and T'ai Chi Ch'uan. He lives in Portland, Oregon.

Winnie ille Pu

Latin edition translated by Dr Alexander Lenard
With original line drawings by E.H. Shepard

The full text of A. A. Milne's *Winnie-the-Pooh*
translated into Latin.

Who can resist attempting, even with basic schoolbook Latin,
to read this rendering of Milne's classic story about
'est optimus ursus mundi' – the best bear in all the world.

Greeted by *Punch*, when it was first published in 1960,
as 'a real don's delight'.

Hungarian born Dr Alexander Lenard printed a hundred
copies of *Winnie ille Pu* in Sao Paulo, Brazil.

'The parents of good students (of Latin) will buy the book
for their children as a gift,' wrote Alexander Lenard to
publishers to encourage them to publish his book.
'The parents of bad students will buy it so their children will
develop a liking for Latin. People who have studied Latin will
buy it so that they finally have a use for their Latin.'

Domus Anguli Puensis

Latin edition translated by
Brian Gerrard Staples
With original line drawings by E.H. Shepard

The full text of A.A. Milne's *The House at Pooh Corner* translated into Latin.

By representing A. A. Milne's puns, special use of words and all the Hums in a translation that reflects Milne's style, Brian Staples shows how it is possible to use correct and acceptable Latin to very good advantage. This will appeal not only to Latin students, but also to those fond of language and Winnie-the-Pooh.

Here are Pu, Porcellus, Ior, Lepus and Tigris, living happily in the Hundred Acre Wood in the language of Tacitus and Virgil.

Brian Staples translated *The House at Pooh Corner* into Latin when he was recovering from a stroke in 1979. For this work he received The Life After Stroke Award.

Say it Again, Pooh

Compiled by Brian Sibley

*With original line drawings by E.H. Shepard,
and full colour illustrations*

Despite being a Bear of Very Little Brain, Winnie-the-Pooh
has managed some startling Thoughts and said
some Extraordinary Things.

This very Useful Book contains the collected thoughts of
Winnie-the-Pooh and his friends from the Hundred Acre
Wood. Here you will find not only Wit and Wisdom, but
also an Abundance of Useful Information,
Sustaining Thoughts, Remarks and Observations.

Brian Sibley is an author, editor and broadcaster.
He has lectured and written on the subject of
Winnie-the-Pooh and his creators.